THE SACRIFICIAL
INTERPRETATION OF
JESUS' ACHIEVEMENT
IN THE NEW TESTAMENT

THE SACRIFICIAL INTERPRETATION OF JESUS' ACHIEVEMENT IN THE NEW TESTAMENT

Historical Development
and Its Reasons

by
Tibor Horvath, S.J.

Philosophical Library
New York

Contents

v

Introduction

This study begins with the supposition that the first understanding that the early Christians had of the person and role
of Jesus would not have been connected with the idea of
sacrifice (cf Mk 8,32; 16,22; Lk 24, 25-26).[1] Not being a
priestly community, they would not have interpreted his
achievement primarily in such terms. Since they did not come
from priestly families, sacrifice would not have occurred to
them as the first and most evident concept in the light of
which they would spontaneously have interpreted the events
of Jesus' life and to which they would have related all that
they were able to understand about it. The importance of
sacrifice, especially in the form with which their Jewish
background made them familiar would not have been so
relevant in their religious thought that it would have won
their loyalty to Christ. It is quite improbable that any of
Jesus' disciples would have been drawn to his following out of

1

a desire to become priests of a new and better sacrificial rite, or of a more perfect sacrifice. The institutional priesthood of Israel was out of their reach, and Jesus could not have intended to create such priestly community.

It seems much more likely that the first disciples gave their adherences to Jesus because they, in some sense, realized that he was the man most highly favored by God (cf Mk 6,51). Quite naturally they entertained their own wishes and expectations in this regard; but they still showed themselves ready to accept what God offered them in Jesus (cf Jn 6,68-69). Fundamentally they were convinced that since Jesus was favored by Yahweh, as long as they remained with him no ill could befall them that would bring upon them Yahweh's condemnation.

According to the Synoptic [2], Pauline [3] and Johannine [4] sources, Jesus' work and all what he offered to his followers and through them to the world, in one word Christ event, was understood originally not as sacrifice but rather an action of moving from the present situation to somewhere else. Such an understanding of Jesus' work as "moving from - to", is, indeed, in the line of the first experience of Jesus in the resurrection-event, as passage from the realm of death to that of life. It was the resurrection event that focused the attention of the early Christians upon the death of Jesus and upon its meaning. Once they experienced Jesus as risen and alive they inevitably asked themselves, Why did he have to die? The question about the *why* of Jesus' death conditioned as it was by the experiences of his resurrection raised in turn the further question about the *why* of his life.

Now it is noteworthy that in seeking an answer to these questions and in dealing with people of other nations and with new situations, the first Christians came to the conclusion that by applying the notion of sacrifice to the life and death of Jesus, the enigma of that life and death became more intelligible and brought the risen Christ and his message closer to the world. They at once felt that in this way they could better understand and explain what the event of the risen Christ really meant. They began, in fact, to apply the term, sacrifice, not only to Christ [5], but also to the life of his followers [6], and to their cultic celebration [7], viz., the breaking of bread, and so too they began to develop a theology of sacrifice.

The statistical distribution of sacrificial terms and of their application to Jesus indicated that the Pauline and Johannine theologies, each in its own way, were more inclined than that of the Synoptic to interpret the achievement of Jesus in a sacrificial sense. The same listing also shows that sacrificial terms are applied far more often to Jesus' life than to that of his followers, or to the Eucharistic celebration. Although it appears unquestionable that the New Testament writers were aware of the sacrificial implications of Jesus' achievement, yet their usage of sacrificial terms and the context in which they used them, raise many questions.

Why did they consider it indispensable for an adequate understanding of his achievement? Furthermore, how did they relate the interpretation of Jesus' work as sacrifice to other interpretations, such as redemption, salvation, purification, expiation, reconciliation, justification etc.? What is the meaning of the sacrificial terms used by the New Testament writers? What is the relationship between the sacrificial interpretation of Jesus' life, that of the life of his followers and that of the Eucharistic celebration? How do these three relate to each other? What are the reasons for the sacrificial interpretation of Jesus' achievement, and for its historical development in the New Testament?

In order to give an answer to these questions, the present study is divided into two parts: 1) the sacrificial interpretation of Jesus' achievement in the New Testament books; 2) the pre-history of this interpretation.

3

1. Sacrificial Interpretation of Jesus' Achievement in the New Testament Books.

One consequence of the Catholic-Protestant debate about the nature of the Eucharistic celebration was that in the New Testament theology of sacrifice too much prominence has in the past been given to the problem of the Last Supper. The questions which prompted research were most likely the following: Is the Last Supper presented in the New Testament as sacrifice? Was it a true Jewish Passover ceremony, or was it rather a rite inspired by *Ḥaburah,* or by *Zikkārôn.?* What is the Last Supper's relation to the Cross?

The theology of sacrifice presented in the New Testament, however, seems to be more comprehensive than these questions would suggest. The vocabulary of New Testament sacrificial terms (see notes 5-7) suggests that a theology of New Testament should include not only the Eucharistic celebration, but also the Christian life seen as sacrifice, as well as the Jesus event viewed as an organic unit.

Moreover, once the Christ event, and in particular his life and death, the life and death too of Jesus' followers, and the Last Supper celebration are all designated as sacrificial, an adequate understanding of the meaning of those terms will demand not so much an abstract consideration of the words in their Old Testament or in their extra-biblical context, but above all a detailed analysis of the New Testament reality that underlies these designations. Instead of adapting the Christ event to an a priori term, the term should be adapted to the reality presented by New Testament writers and should investigate why they interpret that reality eventually in sacrificial terms. Since none of the New Testament books can be considered a treatise on the nature and meaning of sacrifice, but rather as an explanation of the meaning of Jesus' life and death, as well as that of his followers, instead of analysing the Christ event in the light of the notion of sacrifice in general, the sacrificial terms found in the New Testament books should be analysed in the light of the Christ event.

This is precisely what we shall now try to do. We shall first see how the meaning of the life and death of Jesus and that of his followers is presented in the different books of the New Testament, and ask why the authors occasionally interpret that meaning sacrificially.

New Testament Greek, as well as classical Greek, does not have a generic term like the Latin "sacrificium" for all kinds of sacrifice. Before a detailed study, therefore, is made of the individual books of the New Testament, it will be in order to list all the New Testament terms which, we believe, have sacrificial implications, and to indicate the use made of them there in both Christian and non-Christian or in profane contexts.

A. SACRIFICIAL TERMS AND THEIR USE IN THE NEW TESTAMENT

For the New Testament books we found the following terms applied in one way or other to the Christ event:

θυσία, θύω (παραδίδωμι, ἀπολύτρωσις, ἀγοράζω);
θυσιαστήριον, τράπεζα; προσφορά; ὁλοκαύτωμα;
σπένδομαι; ἱλασμός; ἀμνός, ἀρνίον; Πάσχα, ἄζυμος;
αἷμα τοῦ Χριστοῦ, αἷμα τῆς διαθήκης

1) **θυσία, θύω (παραδίδωμι, ἀπολύτρωσις, ἀγοράζω)**
The Greek noun θυσία which is applied by Paul to Christ
(Eph 5,2; cf Heb 7,27; 9,26; etc), in the Synoptics refers only
to the Old Testament sacrifices in a critical sense (Mt 9,13;
12,7; Mk 12,33; Mk 9,49 is not considered as authentic). The
other occurrences in Lk (2,24; 13,1) also refer to the Old
Testament ceremonies but without further evaluation.
The verb θύω is used by the Synoptics six times. Four
times it means the slaughter of animals for banquets (Mt
22,4; Lk 15,23.27.30) and twice, the immolation of the Passover lambs (Mk 14,12; Lk 22,7).
The author of the Acts of the Apostles uses θυσία in the
same way as the Synoptics. The noun occurs twice signifying
the sacrifices of the Old Testament (7,41.42); and the verb
twice means the ordinary killing of an animal for food
(10,13;11,7) and twice, pagan sacrificial killing (14,11.13).
Paul is the first who makes Christian use of θυσία, though
he knows its pagan use as well (1 Cor 10,28). The noun is
applied once to Christ (Eph 5,2) and three times to the lives
of Christ's followers (Rom 12,1; Phil 2,17; 4,18). The verbal
form is applied once to Christ's activity (1 Cor 5,7) and once
to pagan cultic functions (1 Cor 10,20).
It is noteworthy that in 1 Cor 10, 19-22, Christians are
spoken of as having cup, table and communion but not also
θυσία, as do the pagans (1 Cor 10,28). Here what Paul is
considering directly is the breaking of bread, rather than the
violent death of Christ on Calvary. On the other hand, in
chapter 5 he applies the term θυσία to Christ's death. In that
chapter he asks the Corinthians to expel from their midst a
man who has committed incest, and the reason that he gives
is that they are the unleavened bread of sincerity, because of
Christ's Paschal immolation. So it is not sacrifices to idols and

7

the breaking of bread of 1 Cor 10, 19-22 that here remind Paul that Christ has been immolated as the Passover victim, but the need of casting out an evil-doer from the community. It is not the liturgical connection between the feast of unleavened bread and the feast of Passover that turns Paul's mind to the idea of Christ's immolation, but rather the incompatibility between the new and the old yeast. The old must be rooted out (αἴρω, ἐκκαθαίρω, ἐξαίρω 1 Cor 5,2.7.13) since the New Passover has begun. The idea is confirmed in Rom 12,1 where the term θυσία is applied to the Romans who are asked to give up the old by changing themselves into the new. They should not model themselves on the behaviour of the world, but be remade and transformed (Rom 12,2). The new behaviour is described in vv 3-21 as humility and charity towards every man, including even their enemies. The living sacrifice of the Romans is therefore nothing else than giving up hatred in order to be transformed into the charity of Christ, who became a "sacrifice" (Eph 5,2) by giving himself up for the faithful. For this reason all the external manifestations of faith, the obedient surrender of the Philippians to God (Phil 2, 17), as well as the money they gave to Paul, can be called θυσία (Phil 4,18 with 4,15 and 2 Cor 11,8).

Indeed the term θυσία is connected with παραδίδωμι, which stands for θυσία as its epexegesis (Eph 5,2) or its substitutional synonym (Rom 4,25;8,32; Gal 1,4;2,20; 1 Tim 2,6; Tit 2,14). Not only did the Son give himself up (Gal 1,4, 2,20, 1 Tim 2,6; Tit 2,14) but also the Father gave up His Son for men (Rom 4,25;8,32) and for their sins (Gal 1,20; 1 Tim 2,6; Tit 2,14). In this sense of παραδίδωμι, it is not man to God, but rather God who is "sacrificing" to man.

The verb παραδίδωμι is also further connected with the terms λύτρον, ἀντί-, and ἀγοράζω. According to Tit 2,14 Jesus gave himself up for men to redeem (λυτρόω) them from all iniquity and make them his own (see also 1 Tim 2,6).

The redemption means forgiveness of sin (Eph 1,7; Col 1,14) in the present and redemption of the body, viz., resurrection, in the future (Rom 8,23). The verb παραδίδωμι is connected with λύτρον in Mk 10,45, where the metaphor "ransom" might support the theory of substitution, translating ἀντὶ πολλῶν by "instead of many". Since it is never said to whom the ransom is paid, the real meaning would be like that in Tit 2,14, viz., through Jesus man is redeemed, made to belong to God and not just to himself.

To this idea of the payment of a ransom belongs also the idea of ἀγοράζω (1 Cor 6,20;7,23; Gal 3,13;4,5), where again not the means of payment, but the end is emphasized, viz., the love of God, who by giving His Son up "sacrificing" to man, brought it about that man and God are reunited in love.[8]

Sacrifice (θυσία), giving up (παραδίδωμι), and redemption (λυτρόω) are correlated terms in Paul. θυσία is used when the action moves towards God, and παραδίδωμι when it moves from God to man. Apparently Paul did not want to apply the term θύω to God, though the idea he tried to communicate was a sort of God sacrificing himself for men. The redemption further indicates not only the result of God's sacrifice, viz., man's belonging to God, but also the costly way God freed man from sin and from self.

The author of the letter to the Hebrews knows all the uses of θυσία we have found so far (Old Testament sacrifices, nine times: 5,1;7,27;8,3;9,9.29;10,5.8.11;11,4; the sacrifice of Christ on the cross: 9,26;7,27;10,12; the sacrifices of the followers of Christ:13,15.16). In addition to this he introduces a new sense by extending it to the heavenly activity of Christ (9,23). This heavenly sacrifice does not consist in a renewed suffering of Christ, but in his appearance in the presence of God on behalf of those who believe in him. Thus the meaning of θυσία is related to the meaning of appearing ἐμφανίζω, φανερόω vv.24.26, but as something distinct from his man-

9

ifestation of himself in his second coming (cf ὁράω in v.28). The noun θυσία occurs in the first letter of Peter only once (2,5). The new people of God offer powerful spiritual sacrifices to God through Christ. The λογικός of Rom 12,1 is changed here into πνευματικός as a more meaningful term for the Hebrew mind, indicating Yahweh's powerful action within man and distinguishing the θυσία of the new people of God from that of the old.

2) θυσιαστήριον, τράπεζα

θυσιαστήριον a form derived from θυσία is found seventeen times in the New Testament. Thirteen times it means the altar in the Temple (Mt 5,23.24; 23,18-35; Lk 1,11; 11,51; Rom 11,3;1 Cor 9,13; 10,18; Heb 7,13; Jm 2,21); three times the altar in the vision of the book of Revelation, where those who were slain for Christ will remain until the coming of Christ (Rev 6,9;8,3.3). Once it is applied to Christ, who is the living altar through whom the sacrifice of praise is offered (Heb 13,10). The faithful therefore should not use the altar of intercession in the temple, since they can offer this sacrifice of praise through Christ. The altar of Heb 13,10 is most likely not the table of the Eucharistic meal, but the cross, since the sacrifices mentioned in vv 11-12 are sin-offerings, which usually are burnt outside the camp. The term which refers to the Eucharistic table is τράπεζα a term which can mean any kind of table: a banquet table (Mt 15,27; Mk 7,28; Lk 16,21; Acts 6,2;16,34; Rom 11,9); or the table of the money changers (Mt 21,13; Mk 11,15; Lk 19,23: Jn 2,15); or the table with the bread of the Presence in the temple (Heb 9,2 with Lev 24, 5-9); the table used at the Last Supper (Lk 22,21); the banquet table in the kingdom of Christ when the apostles will judge the twelve tribes of Israel (Lk 22,30). In one instance it means the table used by the early Christians in their Eucharistic assembly (1 Cor 10,21): just as the pagans in their sacrificial banquet partake at the table of demons, so the Christians partake at the table of the Lord and will become partners with him.

3) προσφορά

The noun occurs nine times in the New Testament. Four times it signifies the offerings of the Old Testament (Acts 21,26; 24,17; Heb 10,5.8). Four times it is applied to Christ, who gave up himself for the Ephesians not only as θυσία but also as προσφορά, an offering whose fragrance is pleasing to God (Eph 5,2). The offering of his body (Heb 10,10-18) was an offering made once for all for the sins of all mankind. Rom 15.16 applies it to Jesus' followers.

The verbal form of προσφορά is more frequent. It is used forty-six times. In nineteen cases it is used in a profane context with the meaning of presenting some one or something to some one. Twenty-one instances concern the offerings of the Old Testament. Only six instances refer to Christ, who offered prayers and entreaty during his life (Heb 5,7) and then offered himself once and for all (Heb 7,27; 9,14.25.28) for the sins of men (Heb 10,12). All these instances are to be found in the Letter to the Hebrews.

4) ὁλοκαύτωμα

The term "holocaust", a sacrificial burnt offering, is never applied to Christ. All three instances refer to holocausts of the Old Testament (Mk 12,33; Heb 10,6.8). This is surprising since Heb 13,11-12 seems to suggest the idea. Nevertheless Jesus is not called "holocaust".

5) σπένδωμαι

The noun σπονδή, - libation, a kind of drink offering, - does not occur in the New Testament writings. Its verbal form occurs only twice and in both cases it is said of Paul's apostolic life (Phil 2,17; 2 Tim 4,6). The apostle pours out his life as a libation for the faithful, and he feels that it is being slowly exhausted for their sake.

11

6) ἱλασμός

The verbal form occurs twice in the New Testament. In Luke the tax-collector asks God to be propitious to him, or appeased for he is a sinner (Lk 18,13). In Heb 2,17, the direct object of Christ's action is not God but sin. It means the removal of some barrier between God and man (cf Eph 2,14: dividing wall of hostility). Two derivatives from the verb, viz., ἱλασμός (1 Jn 2.2; 4,10), ἱλαστήριον (Rom 3,25), are applied to Christ. The latter term also signifies once the throne of mercy in the Temple (Hb 9,5). God made Christ His instrument for expiating sin; through him He takes sin away (1 Jn 2,2; 4,10). Christ is the sign of God's justice and of His mercy, and also the reason for His forbearance (Rm 3,25).

In the Septuagint ἱλαστήριον translates the Hebrew *Kapōret*, which covered the Ark. The root, *Kipper*, cannot be explained merely as substitution in the penal sense. Originally, it extended to any kind of removal of supernatural danger to a person under tabu and to the atonement that permitted the person to return to the body of society.[9] The statement that Jesus is propitiation demands the identity of the one offering propitiation and the victim offered. For in the New Testament propitiation is never associated, as it is in the Old Testament, with animal sacrifices (i.e. of bulls, goats, etc: Ex. 29,36; Rev. 4,20; 16,9-10), or with the payment of money (Ex 30,16), or with the burning of incense (Num 16,47) or with prayer (Ex 32,30), but solely with Christ himself (cf Hb 9,24 et passim). As forgiveness of sin, propitiation implies Yahweh's communion with His people, their reconciliation with Him and His good favor towards them. Jesus is their ἱλαστήριον for he has taken away the obstacles to reconciliation between God and men. The meaning, however, cannot be reduced simply to the appeasement of God's anger, even though the idea of anger, enmity and hatred is still implicit in the term.

12

7) ἀμνός, ἀρνίον

ἀμνός is always applied to Christ. In Acts 8,32 and Jn 1,29.36, it is the suffering servant (cf Is 53,7), and in I Pet 1,19, the Paschal Lamb without mark and blemish (Ex 12,1ff) that is in the author's mind. In Jn 19,36, the author is most likely thinking of the Paschal Lamb, though he does not there use the term expressly.

Instead of ἀμνός, the book of Revelation uses the term ἀρνίον which means a young lamb. In Jn 21,15 (the only instance of the use of the same term outside the book of Revelation) it is applied to Christ's followers, but in the book of Revelation it is always applied to Christ with but one exception, 13,11, where it designates the second beast, which, having two horns like a lamb, will delude the inhabitants of the earth. Probably the author did not have so much in mind the suffering, obedient servant of Yahweh as the Paschal Lamb of the Eucharistic celebration. The conjunction of the terms Lamb and wedding supper (19,7.9) indicates that the Paschal supper is already seen as the feast of the heavenly kingdom. Jesus Christ is the Lamb (6,1.16;14,1.4.4.10; 15, 3;21,14.44.23.27; 22,1.3), which, though as a young lamb (cf Ex 12,5) it had been killed (5,6;13,8), now receives all power and wealth, wisdom and might, honour, glory and praise (5,8.12.13;7,10;17,14). He is no longer the one *who is crushed*, but the one who crushes his enemy (12,11;17,14), who takes vengeance upon the kings of earth (6,16). Paradoxically, the Lamb shepherds his people (7,17) and his spouse (19,7.9;21,9) and saves them for adoring the false Christ (13,8).

Jesus, unlike the apostles (Mt 10,16), Paul (Rom 8,32), the faithful (Jn 10,15) or the false prophets (Mt 7,17) is never called πρόβατον (sheep).

8) Πάσχα and ἄζυμος

In the Synoptics, in John's Gospel and in the Acts Πάσχα and ἄζυμος might mean either the feast day (Mk 14,1.1.12;

13

Mt 26,2.17; Lk 2,41;22,1.7; Jn 2,13; 2,23; 6,41;11,55;12,1;13, 1;18,39; 19,14; Acts 12, 4.3; 20,6) or the Passover meal (Mk 14,12.14; Mt 26,17.18,19; Lk 22,8.11.13.15; Jn 18,28) both including the idea of immolation or sacrifice (Mk 14,1;Lk 22,7). However it is never, in this instance, applied to Christ himself, as it is in Paul's letter to the Corinthians.

According to 1 Cor 5,7 Christ is the Πάσχα of the believers, who in turn are ἄζυμος, the new dough. The Jewish passover, however, is not mentioned in Paul, as it is in Heb 11,28.

9) αἷμα τοῦ Χριστοῦ, αἷμα τῆς διαθήκης

αἷμα τοῦ Χριστοῦ is perhaps the New Testament term that is most directly sacrificial. In general, blood means death (Mt 23,30.35.35; Lk 11,50,51; 13,1; Mt 27,4.6.8.24.25; Acts 1,19;5,28; 22,20; Rev 6,10;16,3.4) disease (Mk 5,25.29; Mt 9,20; Lk 8,43.44), extreme anxiety and fear of eschatological times (Lk 22,44;18,6;20,26). On the day of Yahweh it will appear as the sign of death not only on earth (Acts 2,19) but also above in the sky, where even the moon will turn into blood (2,20; cf Rev 6,12). It will inundate the moon (Rev 6,12) and flood the earth up to the height of a horse's bridle (Rev 14,10). Even the waters will be turned into blood (Rev 11,6;16,4). As punishment and vengeance (6,10; 19,2), one who has shed blood, will have to drink blood (Rev 16,6; cf Jn 6,54) and to get drunk with blood, like the women of abomination (Rev 17,6; 18,24). In composition with σάρξ it means the weakness of human nature that cannot understand and acknowledge that Jesus is the Son of the living God (Mt 16,17; Jn 1,13), since it is under the slavery of death (Heb 2,14).

Unlike any other blood, the blood of Jesus brings about union with God, purification, and redemption and therefore can become man's drink (cf Jn 6,53.54.55.56).

Indeed in the New Testament writings there is a progressively developing theology of the blood of Jesus.

14

The Synoptics present Jesus' blood as the blood of the covenant (Mt 26,28; Mk 14,24; Lk 22,20; cf Ex 24,8; Zach 9,11) poured out for many. Matthew further determines that it is to be shed for many for the remission of sins (Mt 26,28), and thus combines Ex 24,5-8 (cf also Gen 15,7-8) with Ex 30,10; Lev 14,4-7; 16,1-34 (cf Lev 8,15.19;17,11). Such a tradition is reflected in Heb 9,19-22. Consequently Jesus' blood as the blood of the covenant establishes union between God and man and, as expiatory blood, has the power of purifying and of forgiving sins (cf Lev 14,4-7; Lev 16,1-19;17,11.). Blood is expiatory, it atones because life is in it. Thus Matthew's "theology of blood" implicitly contains John's theology about Jesus' life-giving blood.

A new development appears in the Acts of the Apostles. The blood by which the Church had been brought into being is called God's blood (20,28). The blood of every creature, indeed, belongs to God (Gen 9,4-6; Lev 1.5;3,17), but none as much as the blood of Jesus, who is the servant of God (Acts 3,13;8,37).[10] Through Jesus' blood, which is more God's own (τοῦ ἰδίου) than any other (e.g. the blood of oxen, etc.) or any other animal, God brought about a covenant union that united God and man indissolubly.

Paul further develops the idea of Jesus' blood as the means of achieving union, redemption and remission of sins. His description of the Lord's supper seems, in a certain sense, simpler than that of the Synoptics. Unlike what he says about the bread (1 Cor 11,24), he does not speak of Jesus' blood being poured out either for the faithful (Lk), or for the many (Mk and Mt) for the remission of sins (Mt). The blood is seen rather as the blood of the covenant that binds the faithful until the second coming of Christ. What is original in Paul is that he sees between the bread and cup, and the body and blood of the Lord, such a union that by unworthily (eating and drinking) one cannot but profane thereby the body and blood of Christ (1 Cor 11,27). Anyone who refuses to see, as Paul does, the inseparability between the bread and cup of the Lord and his body and blood, and consequently does not distinguish (διακρίνω) the bread and cup of the Lord from any other bread and cup, - such a man will necessarily be judged (κρίνω) and set apart by the same bread and cup of the Lord (1 Cor 11,29). In other words, if one does not want to be cut off from the covenant-life, one has to cut oneself off from the world (outside the covenant) (cf Eph 2,12-13). The same idea of inseparability is expressed in 1 Cor 10,16. No one can share in the cup of blessing without blood of Christ. Thus the bread and the cup of the Lord are the symbol of the new, definitive and unbreakable convenant of God, brought about by the special unitive power of Jesus' blood.[11]

The most far reaching description of the inseparability of the cup of the Lord and his blood will be given by John, who says that drinking the cup means drinking the blood of Christ (Jn 6,53), and that Jesus' blood is real drink (6,54). Because of this inseparability the properties of wine (such as its being a drink) can be predicated of the blood of Christ. Such a statement by itself, in any context, could not be anything else than blasphemous to a Jew for they were repeatedly forbidden by God to drink blood (cf Jn 6,66-70).

In addition to its unitive function, Paul ascribes other functions to Jesus' blood. It has a redemptive function, and also a revelatory one.

The role of Jesus' blood is like that of faith. As by faith, justification (Rom 3,28,30; Gal 2,16; 3,8.24) is given to man so too, by the blood of Jesus is given redemption (ἀπολύτρωσις) which means forgiveness of sin (Eph 1,7) together with reconciliation of all things with God (ἀποκαταλλάσσω) and peace (εἰρηνοποιέω) with all (Col 1,20,22). Redemption is to be received by faith in the blood of Christ (Rom 3,24-25); for man is justified in his blood (Rom 5,9) in which Christ brought near those who were once far apart, breaking down the dividing wall of hostility (Eph 2,13-16). This efficient causal influence belong-

16

ing to Jesus' blood in redemption, remission of sin (Eph 1,7) and propitiation (Rom 3,25) is expressed in Paul by διά and in reconciliation and justification, by ἐν (Rom 5,9; Eph 2,13).

Finally for Paul the blood of Christ has, as well, a revelatory function. It reveals not only God's wrath, righteousness and forbearance (Rom 3,25-26;5,9) but also His love for men, for it was in Christ's own blood that He justified man (Rom 5,8-9). This revelatory function of the blood will be specially emphasized by John.

Paul's idea that the redemption and justification of men were accomplished by God, at a great cost, is also expressed in 1 Pet 1,17-18. The followers of Jesus are ransomed not with perishable things, such as silver and gold, but with the precious blood of Christ. From this the author deduces the singular vocation of the apostle of Christ. An apostle of Christ is chosen and commissioned for "the sprinkling of Jesus' blood" in order to extend the domain of the New Covenant (1 Pet 1,2) by activating the peace-making power of his blood.

The author of the letter to the Hebrews has a well developed theology concerning the blood of Jesus. All that had been said in the Old Testament about the function of blood is true only of Jesus' blood. It has the power to cleanse and to sanctify (9,7.12.13.21.22; 10,4.29;13,11), as well as to confirm the covenant (9,19.20; 19,20;11,28;12,24). Since blood belongs to God, it speaks and pleads with Him (12,24; cf Gen 4,10), therefore God will come to redeem it. Wherever blood is, there God is present. Blood implies, therefore, His presence. Now since Jesus' blood belongs to God much more than the blood of any other man, there is no blood which signalizes more perfectly the presence of God than Christ's blood. Consequently his blood purifies *(kippēr:* 9,12.13.14) the human conscience. It changes a sense of guilt into an awareness of holiness (cf 9,9.13.14; 10,2.22;13,18) it sanctifies (10, 19-25;13,13) and establishes a new covenant (9,18;13,20). Jesus' shedding of his blood is seen not only as ʿōlāh (burnt sacrifice) but also as *zebaḥ* (communion sacrifice: 13,10), as well as *ḥaṭṭā't* (expiatory sacrifice for sin:13,11-13 etc) and *kippēr* (9,14).

Finally, like Christ, so too the Christians have to offer their blood, by resisting to the point of shedding it in their struggle against sin (12,4).

As we have already noted, John presents the blood of Jesus as drink in the real sense of the word ("unless you eat the flesh of the Son of man and drink his blood ---- my blood is real drink" Jn 6.53-56). Here not only Jesus himself, but his blood is expressly understood as *zebaḥ* (communion sacrifice), whose function was not so much to purify from sin as to give life, - in which the real meaning of the covenant consists (cf Deut 29,1-30, esp. 30,15-20).

Blood, however, according to John, has not only the power to cleanse and to unite men to God in view of eternal life, but also to reveal that life, and the truth of its reality. In his first epistle John declares (1,7) that the blood of Jesus reveals the way that he enters into the world. He comes not only in water, i.e. with the revelation of the Holy Spirit at his baptism, but also in blood, i.e. through his death on the Cross, where God gave testimony to His Son. (1 Jn 5,6-11). His blood reveals that he has come in very truth. This idea of blood as testimony is also put forward in John's Gospel (15,31). The sign that Jesus has been sent by the Father, and that he has come from heaven, is the blood that issues from his side (Jn 6,30,33; 19,34-37). Only when he is lifted up will men know that he is from God and speaks with God's authority (Jn 8,28; cf 8,30, and 12,32). In Joannine theology, blood seems to possess the revelatory function of the Word of God. John's theology of blood as revelation may quite well have been an answer to a contemporary gnostic conception of revelation. It would appear that at that time an inadequate concept of the Word of God could be countered only by relating it to the blood shed on the cross at the death of Jesus. It would be the only safeguard against an ambiguous concept of divine revelation and alone would ensure that it was understood as a living and life-giving reality, and not merely a doctrine about life.

The concept of blood as revelation is known also to the author of the book of Revelation. Christ's blood betokens remission of sin since in (ἐν) his blood the elect were washed and their robes made white (7,14), and their adversaries were vanguished by (διά) it. (12,11). That which brings victory was not only the blood of the Lamb and his word of witness (note the parallelism between blood and τὸν λόγον τῆς μαρτυρίας and death expressed διά... καὶ διά... καί) but the fact that the elect shared in Jesus' death, and their blood too could then become a word of witness (12,11). This was so because Jesus did in fact buy back for God by his blood men of every tribe and language, people and nation (5,9). Blood as witness of the Word of God is once more succinctly expressed in 19,13: The One whose name is the Word of God is clad in a garment dipped in blood.

The vocabulary of New Testament sacrificial terms indicates that all these terms, when applied to the New Testament reality, are used only in a sense analogous to their use in the Old Testament or for any other cultic function to which the term "sacrifice" properly and primarily applies. The New Testament term most akin to that usage is perhaps αἷμα, but even here the blood is that of a man who pours it out for a purpose which need not be the same as that for which sacrificial animals are killed in cultic actions. What the particular purpose is, for which in the New Testament blood is poured out, will be seen in the next section.

B. NEW TESTAMENT SACRIFICIAL REALITY

1) Mark's Theology of Sacrifice

(1) Jesus' life and death

In respect to sacrifice, Mark's Gospel is a source book rather than a theology. Many relevant elements (or items) are stored up in it without being made explicit or connected with one another. Whether or not the author was aware of their sacrificial implications is not clear, but it does not appear in any case that a sacrificial interpretation of them formed the centre of his theological interest.

Mark's purpose was to answer the question, who this man, Jesus, known to be risen from the dead, really was, and to relate what he had done before his resurrection. The author's answer is explicit: the risen Jesus is the Son of God, acknowledged as such in heaven by God the Father, on earth, by the Roman centurion, representative of the greatest power on earth (15,39), in the underworld by the devil (1,34;3,12;5,7). As Son of God, he has inaugurated the Kingdom of God by his preaching and by working miracles that are the signs of its coming (1,14).

It is noteworthy that in Mark's Gospel God displays no signs of anger, as He did in the days of the prophets, but appears rather as well pleased (1,11;9,8). Nor in Mark does Jesus himself manifest any intention of appeasing God's wrath. His purpose rather is just to cure and to save men from disease (1,22,27,32-34; 7,37). With but two exceptions (10, 26;13,13), salvation means for Mark saving life, healing and restoring health (3,4;5,23.28.34;6,56;8,35.35;13,20;15,30.31) and the Father is pleased with Jesus, not precisely because he is going to placate Him through an expiatory death (cf theology of John and Paul), but rather because Jesus is to reveal Him through his preaching and his healing of the sick. He commends himself to the Father not as one to be followed in suffering but as one to be listened to in faith (9,11).

Indeed Mark does not portray either Jesus' life or his death as expiation for sin. Jesus, it is true, asks for repentance (1,15) and he forgives sin (2,5-12;3,28). To do so, however, the Markan Jesus did not have to die. He had the power to do it

20

without suffering. As to the reason why Jesus had to die, Mark does not speak quite clearly. Jesus' life was certainly a life for others: He came to serve (9,35-36) and knew that he would die. According to Mark too, Jesus even foretold his death to his disciples. The reason for it, however, in Mark's account does not stand out clearly.

In 2,18 Jesus says that the bridegroom will be taken away, but he assigns no reason for it. In 8,12, when he refuses to satisfy the demands of the Pharisees, asking for a sign, unlike Matthew, Mark does not mention the sign of Jonah. After Peter's confession in Caesarea, Jesus begins to teach the apostles that the Son of Man must suffer, will be rejected and put to death. But again, it is not said why. No reason is given either in 9,31-32 or in 10,33-34. In 9,2 Jesus asks his disciples why it is that according to the Scripture the Son of Man has to suffer. But the question is left unanswered. Probably Mark himself was not quite sure how to answer it. In 10,38 Jesus is aware that he will drink the cup and be "baptized with the baptism with which I must be baptized", but again, no explicit reason is given by Mark why this must be. He has to go on his way, because so it was appointed for him by the Scriptures (14,21). Nor does the author give any hint that he understood why the Scriptures say so. In 14,36 the term "Scriptures" is replaced by the idea of the will of the Father. It is the will of the Father that Jesus should accept this cup, and thus Scripture reflects the will of the Father. The question, however, why it was the will of the Father that Jesus should die, Mark could not answer.

Certainly there are two instances where the Markan Jesus speaks of his life as being a life for others. In 10,45 he says that the Son of Man gives his life as a ransom for many. The Greek λύτρον found also in the parallel passage in Mt 20,28, is in Mark a "hapax legomenon", and it is not necessarily a sacrificial term which would imply Jesus' death. It is connected rather with unselfish service - a service like that of the slave mentioned in the context (10,41-45). Not the sacrificial, but rather the social impact is stressed, and cannot be disregarded in the context. Jesus therefore seems to be a ransom by becoming the servant of men in order to free them. The other saying that expresses Jesus' awareness that his life is a life for others is found in 14,24. At the Last Supper he says that his blood is poured out for many, but here there is no mention, as in Matthew, of the remission of sins. In Mark, again, the last words on the Cross, quite unlike those of Luke and John, would appear rather as an expression of a frustrated man's meaningless life (15,34). Considered in itself and apart from its actual context, Mk 14,22-24 can, no doubt, have sacrificial implications, but for the author these would not appear to have much relevance. The two basically sacrificial terms, covenant and blood, do not occur elsewhere in his Gospel. Blood, indeed, is mentioned twice, but then only as a sign of disease, viz., in the case of the woman suffering haemorrhage (5,25-29). Mark, it is true, describes the Last Supper in the same way as he describes the miracles of bread (6,30-39; 8,1-10), embodying them in a liturgical form. Yet he does not display clearly the implications of the Passover ceremony. He simply quotes the liturgical text of the Last Supper without highlighting it in any way. His understanding of why and in what sense Jesus was shedding his blood for many cannot be discerned from the Passover ceremony of the Paschal Lamb; it can be gathered rather from the reason why, according to his Gospel, Jesus had to die. In reconstructing Mark's theology of sacrifice, therefore, our fundamental concern should not consist of analysing the sacrificial implications of the Paschal meal, but of asking in what sense the reasons presented by Mark for Jesus' death can ultimately be called sacrificial.

Now, according to Mark, neither the chief priests nor the whole council could find just cause for putting Jesus to death. Pilate knew that Jesus had been delivered to him out of envy, and he decreed his death solely to satisfy the demands of the Jews. But the real reason, according to Mark, is to be found in Jesus' attitude and way of life as it is presented in his gospel. As Mark describes it, there is a growing dramatic tension between Jesus and the world about him which had already begun at the beginning of Jesus' ministry. An analysis of Mark's gospel makes it clear that, in his view, Jesus did not die as an expiation before God but because he was rejected by men. And he was rejected by men, because he first rejected old man-made traditions and way of life which, in Jesus' view, rendered God's word null and void. In other words, Jesus died because he was not ashamed of doing and living in accord with the call given him. Doing always what he had to do, he never for the sake of human tradition made the Word of God null and void (7,13). It would seem, therefore, that the Markan reason why Jesus had to die is to be found in his authentic and uncompromising integrity of character.

Already in 2,15-17 we read that Jesus rejected the traditional separation of the holy and un-holy, the clean and unclean, the just and the sinner. He refused to fast (2,18-20), because he did not want to sew a patch of new cloth on the old. He did not observe the Sabbath (2,23-26), nor the ritual washing of hands before eating or any other purification tradition of the Pharisees. He was against the corban, or gift-dedication to God, because it supplanted God's commandment to doing one's duty to parents.

Mark attaches great importance to the opposition aroused by Jesus in such situations. Already in chapter 2 he says that his failure to observe the Sabbath, scandalized the Pharisees and that they held counsel with the Herodians as to how to destroy him. In 12,12 they went to arrest him because they perceived that the parable that he related was directed against them. His condemnation for blasphemy, that is, for claiming to be the Christ (14,22), as well as the charge that he intended to destroy the temple (14,58;15,29) indicates in

Mark Jesus' unwillingness to conform to their humanly established value-system. As Mark suggests, Jesus was doomed to death because he was not ashamed to speak and to live according to the way of God even at the price of rejecting human traditions. He kept the commandment (ἐντολή) of God and did not teach purely human doctrine (παράδοσις) like the hypocrites who put aside God's commandments in order to cling to human traditions (7,7-9). The reason that Peter is charged with being deceived by Satan, is that he is thinking in man's way and not in God's way (8,33).

Between God's way and man's way there is, according to Mark, irreducible opposition. That is why the only unforgivable sin is to challenge Jesus' integrity by linking him with the unclean spirit (3,29). Indeed Jesus is extremely sensitive to that accusation by the scribes, viz., that he is possessed by Beelzebub. He rejects such an accusation as absurd (3,22-30), and for the same reason he is vehemently opposed to the unclean spirits' proclaiming their recognition of his person (cf 5,18-19). Between Christ and unclean spirits there is utter incompatibility, just as there is also between the kingdom of God and the adulterous and sinful generation of his day (8,34-38). His ways are opposed to any uncleanness: evil thoughts, fornication, adultery, envy, slander, pride, folly (7,21-23; 10,19-22).

Thus it appears, according to Mark, that it was because Jesus gave witness to God and His work, and because nothing, not even death, could prevent him from giving witness that he died. For, unlike men, he never put in the place of God's way any merely human system of values (ἐντολή :7,9; λόγος :7,13; τὰ τοῦ Θεοῦ 8,33; παράδοσις:7,9; 1,13; τὰ τῶν ἀνθρώπων: 8,33)

The incompatibility between the "new" and the "old", between God's eschatological way and man's futile way, is what explains the life as well as the death of the Markan Jesus. It does not perhaps convey the common notion of sacrifice, as it appears in cultic ceremonies. If the notion of sacrifice is to be applied to the life and death of the Markan Jesus, it cannot mean anything but dedication to God's new way as it replaces the old. The sacrificial meaning of Jesus' life and death according to Mark is the recognition and the realization of the new that is to come which demands the death of what has been. It is essentially oriented to the new kingdom of God, and this entails discarding and casting out of the old leaven.[12] In such a general context the Eucharistic words concerning Jesus' life (shedding his blood for many) can mean neither banquet nor commemoration of the Passover, but Jesus' complete dedication to being what God wants him to be. The bread and wine, which by the Eucharistic word is declared to be his body and blood, can only be the symbol of his life, and it is as such that, by sharing, in the authenticity of the symbolized reality, they manifest the incompatibility between God's new way and man's old way.

(2) *The life and death of Jesus' followers*

In Mark's account, the meaning of the life and death of Jesus' followers does not differ much from that of Jesus' life and death. The difference there is only in the fact that they do not, like Jesus, follow God and the way of God but only the way of Jesus. Just as for Jesus there is no compromise between the Father's way and man's, so for Jesus' followers there is none between the way of Jesus and the way of the world. If any one follows Jesus, says Mark, he has to take up his cross and lose his life for Jesus' sake. As Jesus was not ashamed of God and of His words, so Christ's followers are not to be ashamed of Jesus and of his words in a wicked and godless age (8,34-38). Like Jesus, the disciples too, are not sent to sacrifice, but to preach and heal (3,15;6,12;16,15.2) and to bear witness to Christ before governors and kings. For this they will be hated and put to death, just as Jesus was, who died because he was faithful to his Father and to His kingdom (13,9-13).

25

Since preaching, teaching and faith in Jesus means healing and salvation (cf 2,5;6,6;10,51;11,20-23;16,15-18), the disciples should never abandon the new kingdom for the old. The leaven of the old cannot be used by them (8,14-21). Everything that is old, - even one's eye, or foot, (9,42-48), must be given up for the new (10,17-27), because the new and old are incompatible (4,1-32). It is understandable, therefore, that, not as in Assyrian worship and that of the Old Testament (Lev 2,13), it is not the meal, but Jesus' followers themselves, who are to be salted. Since salt, like fire, not only purifies and consumes what is corruptible, but also preserves what is new (Lev 2,13; Ez 16,4;2 King 2,20), it becomes the symbol of the the purifying, consuming and re-invigorating force that the life of Jesus' followers has on the old way of life.[13]

(3) *The Last Supper - Eucharistic celebration*

The Eucharistic celebration itself according to the Markan tradition is not separated from the Passover meal. It happened during the meal, when the Passover lambs were being slaughtered. Would this be a criterion for assigning certain priority in the history of texts, as Marxsen suggests, [14] the Markan text would, then, be prior to Paul, since Paul believes that the celebration with the cup took place after the supper μετὰ τὸ δειπνῆσαι (1 Cor 11,25). According to Mark the disciples were eating when Jesus took some bread. After having said the blessing (εὐλογέω) he gave the bread to his followers with the words: "This is my body". The same he did with the cup: He gave thanks (εὐχαριστέω), gave the cup to his followers with the words: "This is my blood of the covenant, shed for you. I tell you this: never again shall I drink from the fruit of the vine until that day when I drink it new in the kingdom of God" (14,24-25).

The fundamental problem concerning the Last Supper is to explain how Jesus and the early Chruch come to celebrate the Last Supper in the way described in Mark. First of all, unlike the Jewish Passover, the Last Supper celebration is oriented not towards the past, but towards the future. Its main feature is a parting farewell rather than the sacrificial thanksgiving of the Passover. Indeed, unlike the Passover for the Jews, the Last Supper celebration cannot, for Jesus, be conceived as a thanksgiving. Since he was going to his death, the Last Supper could not mean for him salvation, as it did for the first born of the Jews, but rather death, - the fate of the first born of the Egyptians (cf Ex 12,23). Moreover not the Paschal lamb lying on the table, but bread and wine are assumed as the symbol for both his imminent death and the eschatological banquet to come in the kingdom of God. In an extraordinary way the symbolism of the Last Supper moves from the wine to the shedding of blood and then towards a joyous festivity of happiness. Indeed it cannot be stressed enough that the symbolism of the Last Supper is original and supposes a certain creativity in its composition.

The question why the early Church celebrated Jesus' memory in the way described in Mark, cannot be answered as, for example, Marxsen does,[15] by saying that the meal played a special role in the synoptic tradition. It seems that the opposite is true. The meal in Mark appears as something rather incidental (see 1,6;3,20;5,43). Even the meaning of the multiplication of bread was not cultic, but rather that of an act of mercy (6,34;8,2). Indeed in Mark as well as in the Synoptics in general, the tendency is rather to "secularize" the meal, - contrary to the ritual tradition of the Pharisees (cf 2,16;2, 26;7,2.3.4.5). From the merely statistical standpoint, the people of the Markan tradition are portrayed as spending their time not so much by eating as by walking and going from place to place. Thus for example the term ἔρχομαι occurs in Mark 88 times, whereas ἐσθίω only 26 times. Hence there is no reason why the early Church should begin to commemorate Jesus by a meal rather than by a pilgrimage. In the Synoptics, in fact, Jesus' sermons do not resemble table-talk at all. Only after continued observance of the Eucharistic celebration do table-talks develop such as those recorded in Acts 20,7-11 or Jn 13,1-18,1.

Again the representation of wine as the symbol of Jesus' blood, which was to be drunk, must have appeared to any Jew as an abominable rejection of Yahweh's prohibition (cf Gen 9,4; etc.). True, wine as a symbol of blood was not completely unknown to Jewish tradition (cf Sir 50,15); but even as a symbol of blood, wine was to be poured out as a libation and not offered as a drink. Likewise, according to the latest of Jewish rituals, the holocaust, (Lev 23,17-18; Ex 29,38-42) as well as the sacrifices of 'ôlāh and zebaḥ (Num 15,1-16), had to be followed by minḥah, i.e. an offering of flour mixed with oil and a libation of wine. No scholars, however, have tried to represent the Last Supper as a sort of minḥah, related to the holocaust of the cross.

In the Jewish Passover wine did not play a central role. Exodus 12,1-13.15-27 does not mention either wine or cup. In general wine was not related to the cultic celebrations of the Old Testament the way it was in pagan cults. It was considered rather as a danger which might lead to sinful idolatry. Outside cultic celebrations however, wine was considered a symbol of happiness and joy (cf Is 25,6-9). Food and wine were symbols of life, - one who can eat will not die (cf the body of Christ as food giving eternal life: Jn 6,51-58). In the Markan context, too, bread and wine are used not as symbols of sacrifice, but as symbols of happiness and joy. Now the surprising thing is that the ordinary symbols of happiness, viz., wine and bread, here symbolize the shedding of the blood of one who at the same time looks forward to an eschatological banquet in the kingdom of God. In other words death is symbolized by symbols of happiness. In view of the new symbolism it would appear that the Last Supper was the anticipation of the eschatological banquet rather than the commemoration of the Passover.

In virtue of the Eucharistic words the bread and wine are

brought into such a close relation with Jesus' body and blood that these are understood as real nourishment, i.e. food and drink for those invited to the eschatological banquet. Just as the bread and wine were in the "old" visible world, so now Jesus' body and blood will be the symbol of life, happiness and joy in the "new" world. The old happiness symbolized by bread and wine is replaced by new happiness symbolized by Jesus' body and blood. Thus the Last Supper celebration necessarily includes symbolically even the death of Jesus as well as his resurrection.

Such an interpretation of the Last Supper's symbolism corresponds to the Markan interpretation of the meaning of Jesus' life and death. For Mark, Jesus' life and death was seen as a perfect dedication to the way of the Father that rejects anything that would hinder it. The incompatibility stressed by Mark between the "old" and the "new" has been brought to a final climax in Jesus' Eucharistic words. The old symbol is made null and void by the new. From that time Jesus is the real food and drink, i.e. source of the new happiness. Thus the transformation or "transubstantiation" of bread and wine into the body and blood of Christ seems to be implied in the Markan incompatibility between the "old" and the "new". In this context it is easy to understand why that, unlike Paul and Luke, Mark did not feel it necessary to mention Jesus' command concerning the repetition of the Eucharistic celebration as a commemoration of himself.

2) *Luke's Theology of Sacrifice*

(1) *Jesus' life and death*

In many respects Luke's theology of sacrifice is quite similar to that of Mark. Like Mark, Luke does not feel that God the Father is to be appeased and reconciled by Jesus' life and death. The Lukan God is not angry. From the first, rather, he

29

is well pleased (1,30;2,40;3,22;4,35). The greeting of His messengers is constantly: "Do not be afraid" (1,13;1,30;2,10). Jesus' time is a time of God's favor and joy to the whole people (2,10).

It is true that, contrary to Mark, Luke agrees with Matthew that John the Baptist presented the day of the Messiah as a day of anger, retribution and judgment. Nevertheless the purpose of Jesus' life, as well as the reason for his death, is not the forgiveness of sin. Unlike the Matthean Jesus, the Lukan Jesus did not die for the remission of sins (22,19-20). As in Mark, he forgives sins apart from his own suffering and death (5,17-25). The repentance proclaimed by John the Baptist (3,3) is the salutary effect of the miracles of Jesus (10,13). The forgiveness of sin is one of the petitions of the Our Father (11,3.52). Jesus, indeed, seems to be convinced that people without repentance might perish like the Galileans killed by Pilate (13,1-5). Nevertheless, when he talks about the purpose of his life, he does not express it in the terms used by John the Baptist, but rather in those of Simeon: salvation, light and glory, as well as a sign which men will reject (2,29-34).

In Nazareth, Jesus discloses the meaning of his life by quoting Is 61,1-2, viz., to give liberty to the captives, sight to the blind, freedom to the oppressed and good news to the poor (4,18-22). According to 4,13 he came to proclaim the Good News of the kingdom of God and to let people hear the word of God (5,1). For John the Baptist he explains his mission in identical terms: the blind see, the lame walk, lepers are cleansed, the deaf hear and the dead are raised to life, the poor hear the Good News (7,18-22). In one word, the purpose of his life is to live for others, helping men and saving them from all their miseries.

To the question, why Jesus had to die, Luke again, following Mark, has a double answer: first, Jesus had to die because he did not follow the way and the patterns of his contemporaries, and secondly, he had to die because it was so written.

Already the twelve-year old Jesus does not follow his parents' way of thinking, because he has to be busy with his Father's affairs and follow His way (2,49). Later he antagonizes his town-folk by not performing the marvelous deeds they ask for. For this reason they are so enraged that they want to kill him (4,20-30). Again he rejects the devil's temptations, because the suggestions of his tempter are against the way of his Father as recorded for him in the Scriptures (4,4.8.12). Like the Markan, so the Lukan Jesus too is extremely careful to avoid any suspicion that he has some kind of communion with the devil (4,41). This is why he does not let men, from whom devils had been cast out (8,38-39) remain in his company.

Moreover he does not fast and does not keep the Sabbath, and eats with sinners (5,29-6,11;13,10-17). After seeing all this, says Luke, the leaders of the people started to dispute among themselves what they could do with Jesus (6,11). They complained that he welcomed sinners and ate with them (15,1-2;19,7).

Jesus himself feels that the reason that he is rejected by men as a glutton and a drunkard is that they do not recognize God's plan. Men reject him and in turn he rejects all who do not welcome and esteem God's work and his plan (βουλή :Lk 7,30-35). Uncompromisingly, the Lukan Jesus assails anyone who opposes God's plan. He attacks the Pharisees as well as the lawyers because they were scandalized that he did not wash his hands before dinner (11,37-54). He condemns them because they like taking the seats of honour, and because they swallow the property of widows. He calls them fools, for, while outwardly clean, inwardly they themselves are filled with extortion and wickedness, overlooking and neglecting, as they do, justice and the love of God. And when one of the lawyers protests that they too feel insulted by Jesus' words, he condemns them as well; for they have taken away the key of knowledge - they have not gone in themselves and have

31

prevented others from entering the kingdom. After this denunciation the scribes and Pharisees set many traps to catch Jesus out in something he might say.

On the same grounds, the Lukan Jesus blames also the crowds. They can interpret the face of earth and sky, but they cannot interpret their times (12,56). Again, for the same reason, Herod is called a fox (13,32). Indeed, for Luke, Jesus came to cast fire on earth and bring instead of peace, division: division of house against house, division of father against son, etc. (12,49-53).

It is not then surprising that before Pilate Jesus will be accused of inciting people to revolt (23,11). And Pilate without finding any other reason, delivered him up to the demand of the people (23,34). In condemning Jesus, the Sanhedrin followed the same line. Against the convictions of the populace, Jesus dared to confess that he was the Christ, the Son of Man, to be seated hereafter at the right-hand of the Father (22,66-70).

Thus Jesus met death because he would not abandon the way of God for the way of man. Having accepted God's plan he strove to realize it in spite of all opposition. If one calls the life of such a man sacrifice, then sacrifice would mean nothing else than the acceptance of God's plan, whereas the refusal of sacrifice would be equivalent to thwarting or rejecting God's plan and following instead the ways of men. The other Lukan reason for Christ's death further confirms this conclusion.

Luke says that Jesus died because it was so written. Already in 2,34 it is said that Jesus is destined to be rejected by men. After the confession of Peter, Jesus tells to his followers that he has (δεῖ) to suffer and to be rejected and to be raised up on the third day (9,22). But he gives no reason why it must be so. In 9,44-45, Jesus repeats the same prediction, again without any a reason for his Passion. Nevertheless the disciples are blamed by the evangelist for not seeing the reason for it. They were afraid of asking what he meant. It might seem that Luke himself did not know what Jesus meant by his prediction.

Unlike Mark, however, Luke mentions explicitly the sign of Jonah as the sign given to the generation that asks for a sign (11,29). In the third prophecy of the passion, further details are added but again no further explanation is given for it. It is written (18,31-34) since it had been determined (ὁρίζω 22, 22). In v.24 this determination is made equivalent to the will of the Father. Jesus' dedication to his Father's will is expressed also in his last word at the cross: "Father, into your hands I commit my spirit" (23,46). The loud cry of desperation in Mark turned to be in Luke the expression of Jesus' whole life: dedication to his Father's way.

During the Last Supper the reason for Jesus' shedding blood is found in his disciples themselves. His blood is shed not for the remission of sin, but just for his disciples, to whom he gave the cup (22,20). As in his life so in his death Jesus is seen as man for others. After the resurrection the angel confirms that he had (δεῖ) to be handed over to sinful men and be crucified. According to 24,44 Jesus explained in detail to the disciples why Christ had to die according to the Scriptures. Unfortunately, Luke could not find Jesus' homily in his source so his theology of sacrifice does not mark any progress beyond that of Mark.

Nevertheless there is one element in Luke which will be developed in Matthew. In 24,47 the risen Christ opened the mind of the Eleven and their companions to understand the Scriptures, telling them it was written not only that Christ had to suffer, but also that in his name repentance for the forgiveness of sins will be preached to all nations. Matthew will combine the two statements into one: by stating that Christ died for the remission of sins (Mt 26,28). Thus interestingly enough the Matthean tradition reflects more the Pauline theology of sacrifice than the Lukan one.

In brief it is true that the temporal circumstances of Jesus' death viz., its happening at the time of the Unleavened Bread and Passover feast, might have suggested the recognition of Jesus as Paschal Lamb such as it is presented by Paul and John. However, it does not seem that the first Christians (at least those knowing the Markan and Matthean tradition) at once conceived Jesus' life in terms of a passover victim. His life and death was seen much more as definitive dedication to following God's way rather than man's way and this even at the price of life. This is the meaning which is reflected in the life of Jesus' followers as well as in the Eucharistic ceremony described by Luke.

(2) *The life and death of Jesus' followers.*

Just as the way of Jesus' life in Luke's presentation of it appears incompatible with the old way of life, so too does the way of Jesus' followers. What is valued in the eyes of the old world, viz., wealth, self-satisfaction, gaiety, etc., is reprobated, and what is despised by the world is blessed by Jesus. In order to possess the kingdom of God the followers of Jesus are to be poor, hungry, weeping and persecuted. Their reward is not on earth, but in heaven. Though the world hates them, nevertheless they must love the world and grant pardon to the world (6,20-38). The life of Jesus' disciples cannot be like that of the hypocrites who are clean outwardly but unclean inwardly. Their life must rather be like a house built on rock. It can never be shaken (6,39-49), not even by death. To be fit for the kingdom of God they must never look back (9,60-62) and hesitate. Their speech must be open and fearless (12,1-3). They are to be men of complete dedication (12,47) who store up treasure not on earth but in heaven (12,21.33). Self-renunciation, carrying the cross, even though these involve giving up parents, children and life itself (14,25-34) are recommended by Luke to those who are called to be Jesus' disciples. If they are not equal to this, they are at once like salt which has lost its savor, and which cannot be seasoned again. Now if the life of the Christian is to be called sacrifice, for Luke this would mean authenticity and integrity. In a possible Lukan terminology the sacrificial life of Jesus' disciples would be a life in which deeds correspond to words, a life which inwardly as well as outwardly is conformed definitively not to the way of men but to the way of God. In short, the sacrificial life of Jesus' followers would mean that they hear the word of Jesus and do it (6,47) so that their acts indeed overflow from their hearts (6,45). But for some reason Luke did not apply sacrificial terms to the life of Jesus' disciples, as Paul did. Very probably because it would not have made much sense for his readers. Or perhaps because the "Sitz in Leben" of his narrative did not make him at all conscious of the theological value of such a term.

(3) *The Last Supper - Eucharistic celebration*

The Lukan Eucharistic celebration more than that of the other two Synoptics stresses the eschatological aspect of the Last Supper. The Lukan Last Supper is definitively a Last Supper. Jesus longed to eat this supper with the disciples before his death, since he shall neither eat (proper to Luke) nor drink again until the kingdom of God comes (24,14-18).

The double giving of the cup presented in Luke indicates two current traditions in the celebration of the Last Supper: the eschatological one (cf Mark and Matthew) and the commemorative one (cf Paul). Luke, like Mark and Matthew still extolls the eschatological aspect of the Last Supper, but unlike Mark and Matthew he mentions, as Paul does, the commemorative repetition of the celebration. The use of the two cups was mentioned to make clear that the Jewish

Passover and the Last Supper ceremony are to be clearly distinguished, as well as to indicate that the central point for Luke is not so much eschatological expectation as commemoration of Jesus. Indeed the eschatological expectation becomes secondary and connected probably with the first cup, which according to Mishna ritual has been followed by the recital of the part of Hallel-blessing (see Ps 112,1-113,8). After this, according to Luke, Jesus introduced a really new significance which pervaded the whole Last Supper ceremony.

At the moment when the head of the family is supposed to give an explanation of the Passover, Jesus turns the whole celebration into a memorial of himself. Immediately after the bread is distributed he admonishes them: "Do this in memory of me" (22,19). This admonition is repeated in Paul twice (1 Cor 11,24.25) and with the emphasis: "For every time you eat this bread and drink the cup, you proclaim the death of the Lord until he comes" (1 Cor 11,26). In Luke the emphasis is achieved by the shock of Jesus' statement that one of them sitting with him at table will be his betrayer (22,21-23). The bewilderment and questioning that followed Jesus' statements worked in two ways: it made the traditional meaning of the Passover sink into insignificance and at the same time it impressed on the minds of those present the tragic significance of what was about to happen to them.

As to the purpose of Jesus' death, Luke again agrees with Paul informing Mk and Mt: it is ὑπὲρ ὑμῶν and not ὑπὲρ πολλῶν. Jesus gives his body (σῶμα) and pours out his blood (ποτήριον), symbol of death (cf 22,42) for his followers. But it is not said that this will be done for the remission of sins.

Thus the Eucharistic celebration points towards the death of Jesus. Being essentially related to it, it is the symbol, the word or expression of it. It belongs to the cross as the word which explains the meaning of his death in the light of eschatological hope. The death on the cross is to be understood in the words of the Last Supper, which signify proleptically the messianic banquet, and these in turn are to be reinterpreted by the event on the cross.[16]

Taking the celebration of the Last Supper and Jesus' death on the cross together, we can say that according to Luke the death of Jesus is for his faithful disciples, because that was the will of the Father (23,46). But the question why this was the will of the Father and why Jesus had to die for others is not explicitly answered by Luke. Luke is not as explicit on this point as Matthew, Paul or John will be. It is understandable that unlike Paul and John, Luke and the other two Synoptics do not use any explicit sacrificial terms to explain the meaning of the Jesus' event. Their theology is the theology of the simple believer, for whom the will of God, the way of God, is the final answer. Only a theologian inquires about the why of the will of God and looks for some new reason in order to explain the divine will. Paul and John try to elaborate some further understanding of the way of the Lord in order to help Jesus' followers to accept God's will. The concept of sacrifice is one of the notions which they found useful for such a purpose.

3) *Matthew's Theology of Sacrifice*

(1) *Jesus' life and death*

The Markan and Lukan tradition concerning the meaning of Jesus' life and death is known to Matthew. Jesus had (δεῖ: 16,21) to come and perform his task (cf 1,22;2, 5.13.17; 3,3; 4,4.6.7.10.14; 8,17; 11,10; 12,17; 13,14.35; 15,7; 21,4.16.42) as well as to suffer (26,4.54.56) since it was so written and in order to fulfill the will of the Father (26,

37

39.42.45) when the hour came (26,45). The new element in Matthean theology is that this happened for the remission of sins (cf 1,21;26,28).

As in Mark, so in Matthew, the Son of Man has the power of forgiving sins (9,6), but this is more central in Matthew than in Mark and in Luke. Matthew says explicitly that the purpose of Jesus' life and death is to save his people from their sins (1,21;26,28).

As in Mark and in Luke, Jesus' incompatibility with the leaders of his people will lead to his death (cf 15,6;26,61;26, 63-64;27,11). This incompatibility, however, is formulated by Matthew as an inward quality of mercy as opposed to a concern only for external regulations. When Jesus is criticized for eating with sinners and tax collectors, Matthew adds that Jesus demanded of his accusers that they learn the meaning of these words: "What I want is mercy not sacrifice" (9,13;12,7). Consequently if one would apply the term "sacrifice" to the life and death of the Matthean Jesus it would mean a life of mercy and forgiveness even at the price of death.

The element of forgiveness of sins, however, is not fully integrated in the Matthean gospel, as, for example, it is in the theology of Paul. When the Matthean Jesus dies on the cross he does not utter either the Lukan "Father into your hands I commit my spirit" (Lk 23,46) nor the Johannine "It is accomplished" (Jn 19,30). He gives rather, as Mark does, signs of being frustrated and abandoned by God (Mt 27,46).

After the resurrection one would expect that, in accordance with 1,21 and 26,28, the risen Christ would send his disciples to preach repentance and forgiveness of sins. The author, however, seems to be satisfied with the general commission given to them, viz., of teaching men to observe whatever Jesus had commanded (27,20). The reason for the resurrection given by the angel is the word of Jesus. He is risen not because Scripture says so, but because he said so (28,6;cf

16,21-23;17,22-23;20,17-19). No indication is given why he had to suffer according to Scriptures.

(2) *The life and death of Jesus' followers*

·The way of God which forms the pattern of the life of Jesus' followers is described in the Sermon on the Mount. Apparently it reflects the "do ut des" theory of sacrifice. Christ's followers are to be poor, gentle here on earth in order to be rich and happy in the kingdom of heaven. The word and way of God cannot be given up for human customs and worldly values (6,1-12.20). The fundamental idea of the Sermon, however, is that the internal must come first and the external must flow out of the internal (5,17-48; cf 15,10-20). The authentic life of the disciples, like the house built on rock, is unshakable.

The Matthean Jesus, like the Markan and Lukan, demands open, free and fearless speech that faces up even to persecution. He did not come to bring peace but the sword, and to set man against men. Nevertheless there is one thing which the Matthean Jesus demands especially from his followers: mercy and forgiveness. One of the beatitudes refers to those who show mercy (5,7). Reconciliation with a brother shall precede any gift given to the altar (5,23-24). To come to terms with one's opponents is also recommended (5,25). After the Lord's Prayer (Mt 6,12; Lk 11,4), Matthew makes it emphatically clear that if disciples do not forgive others, God will not forgive them the wrongs they have done (6,14-15). Every one has to forgive his brother from his heart (18,35). The two verses of Lk concerning forgiveness of brothers (Lk 17,3-4) are considerably extended by Matthew (cf 18,15-22). Finally Matthew is the only one who relates a parable of Jesus about the tragedy of the unforgiving servant (18,23-35).

It would seem, therefore, that the sacrificial interpretation of the lives of Jesus' disciples would eventually consist in their forgiveness of the sins of others against them. Acting thus, they will be like a city built on a hill, a lamp set on a lampstand, for their good deeds invite the world to praise the Heavenly Father (5,13-16).

(3) *The Last Supper - Eucharistic celebration*

Since Matthew is the only one who affirms explicitly that Jesus' blood is to be poured out for the remission of sins, the view that extols the Eucharist as a sacrifice for sins, will be based mainly on Matthew as its primary source.

Sin in Matthew however cannot be seen as some kind of ceremonial negligence which angers God. Essentially it is injustice committed against man (cf 18,15.21;27,4;12,31; see also the list of sins in 15,19 with its context 15,1-20.) It is a refusal of the way of Jesus' life who preferred to die rather than to kill (cf 26,52-53) since he loved even his enemies (5,43-48; cf also Lk 6,27-36;23,34a). Even the sin against the Holy Spirit is a sin against man, since it is a refusal to accept the Holy Spirit's witness to the Son of Man. For this reason sin against the Holy Spirit cannot be forgiven either in this world or in the next. There is no neutrality in regard to Jesus (12,30). Once faith not in God alone but in Jesus is demanded, the meaning of sin necessarily takes a new turn. It implies a wrong attitude in one's relations to other men, the evil of which God has revealed in Jesus, for Jesus proved that the ways of God differ from the ways of men.

4) *Theology of Sacrifice in the Acts of the Apostles*

(1) *Jesus' life and death*

The author of the Acts of the Apostles goes somewhat

further in explaining the reason of Jesus' life and death and more particularly that of the resurrection.

The meaning of Jesus' life is the fulfilment of the Old Testament blessing of Abraham extended to the whole world (3,25-26,23) and salvation (σωτηρία ; 4,12;11,14;15,11;16, 17.30-31) which means more than physical health (cf e.g. 3,16;14,10). It is life (3,15;11,18;13,46.48). It includes forgiveness (2,38;10,43;13,38) and the promises of the Holy Spirit (2,32-33; cf 1,5;2,4.16-21).

There is however no connection between the remission of sins and Jesus' suffering. It seems that repentance and forgiveness of sins are the result not of Jesus' death but rather of his exaltation, which in turn is due to Jesus' obedience (5,31). Remission of sins means basically being acquitted of every charge of which man could not be acquitted in the Law of Moses (cf 13,39; for this outlook see Gal 2,16;3,10-14.24; Rom 6,7;8,3;10,4). But this acquittal again is a sign of the descent of the Holy Spirit, rather than a direct and immediate effect attributed to Jesus' death (11,15-18). Unlike the reason of death, the reason of Jesus' resurrection is very clear for the author. Being with God, he could not stay in Hades. He had to be raised (2,27-28;3,14;13,30-37) and thus become Lord and Christ (2,36;9,22;18,5.28). In virtue of his resurrection he will judge the whole world on a day fixed by God (17,3). Thus it seems that the resurrection and sitting at the right of God, rather than the suffering and death of Jesus, are seen as the explanatory theological reason of the universal salvific role of Jesus in the world.

For explaining the theological reason of Jesus' suffering and death the author of the Acts of the Apostles is not of great help. Jesus was delivered up according to the definitive plan and foreknowledge of God (2,23-24). Jesus lived and suffered because God wanted it so. The Messiah had to suffer (3,18). The author is convinced that the Old Testament prophecies indicate this divine plan and give the reason for it. But apart from this factual statement no explicit explanation is given which would help us see why God could want such a terrible fate for Jesus. The Jewish people did indeed kill Jesus without knowing what they were really doing. They did so because God wanted it so. Through their ignorance God could fulfil what was foretold, therefore they are not responsible (cf 3,13-18). Even Herod and Pilate conspired with the Gentiles and peoples of Israel in order to do all that was foretold. This idea of foreordination is expressed also by terms common to the Synoptics viz., "Scriptures" (13,29,36;17,2-3), or "Moses" and the "Prophets" (26,22-23.27). It is doubtful, however, that the author really knew why this was the will of God. One example of how the Scriptures foretold that the Messiah had to suffer is given in 8,32-35. The passage quoted from Isaiah, however, gives an indication how the Messiah reacted to his slaughter (sc. like a sheep that showed no resistance) but does not give the reason why he had to be slaughtered. Acts 10,43 again does not afford us much help. The meaning of the prophecy is that everyone trusting in Jesus will receive forgiveness of sins through his name. But the passion is not mentioned in the context as the reason for it.

In the speech of Stephen (7,1-53) the reason for Jesus' death seems to be the incredulity of the Jewish people, who do not obey the prophets. In order to fulfil His promise, viz., to give Israel a homeland, God sends Moses as its leader and prophet. But the people do not accept his leadership (7,35-43). And here is where Stephen seems to make his point. Jesus had to die, because the Jews persecuted all the prophets and so Jesus too (7,51-53). For such an accusation Stephen himself will be killed (7,54-60). It seems, therefore, that according to Acts, ch.7, as well as according to the Synoptics, Jesus was the victim of internal Jewish aberration concerning what the will of God really was, and who was God's real Messenger.

Briefly, Jesus' life and death as presented in the Acts of the Apostles, were fundamentally the fulfilment of the will of God. If we apply the notion of sacrifice to such a life and death, the meaning of the term would be the perfect fulfilment of God's will, and its consequence, the seating of Jesus at the right of God (cf 2,34). The will of God, the essence of Jesus' sacrificial life, is expressed in Luke, for Jesus' followers particularly, by the notion of way of the Lord.

(2) *The life and death of Jesus' followers*

The life of the disciples of the Lord is seen in the Acts of the Apostles as a new "way" (ὁδός: 9,2;18,26;19,9.23;22,4;24, 14.22.44), as the "way of the Lord" (13,10;18,25) and "the way of God" (18,26). Jesus' followers are not like others, but a sort of especially selected sect (αἵρεσις: see 24,5.14;28,22) for whom in Rome, unlike Jerusalem (4,13-14), no one (except the faithful) had a good word to say (28,22). This sect is the community of those who were destined by the will of God to be saved (2,47).

Now this new life (5,19) was a life filled with Holy Spirit (1,5;2,4;2,16-21;38-39). It meant to be baptized in the name of Jesus, the results of which were the remission of sin and the gifts of the Holy Spirit (2,38-39;22,16). Seemingly here we find the first explicit connection between those baptized in the name of Jesus and the remission of sins. But baptism does not here mean suffering, as it did in the Synoptics, but rather being accepted among the disciples of Jesus and having the visible sign of faith in Jesus (8,26-40). Now the manifest sign of faith could be to perform miracles that would impress people (2,4.43;5,12,16;19,11-20), or some extraordinary event that would cause fear and reveal punishment (5,1-11;13,4-12) that would impress the whole Church (5,1;cf 8,9-24).

More concretely, the new way consisted in being faithful to the teaching of the apostles, living in brotherhood, breaking bread and finally in praying (2,41-42). The followers of Jesus, especially in Jerusalem, shared their goods gladly. No one claimed anything for his own use. Everything they had was held in common (2,42-47;4,32-37;5,1-11).

Their prayer was either prayer of petition (8,22-24) especially for forgiveness (8,22-24), or of thanksgiving (28,15) and praise (16,25). Most of them regularly went to the temple daily (2,46) at the time of evening sacrifice (3,1;cf Ex 29,39, 42; Lk 1,8-10; Acts 10,3.30;21,26). Though they had a special meeting place where no one ventured to disturb them, some even performed purification ceremonies and made offerings according to the Law (18,18; 20,22-26) in the Temple itself. Moreover they invoked Jesus' name (2,21.38;3,13-16;9, 14.21;22,16) and witnessed that he was the Lord and Christ (2,36). They did this even at the risk of their lives (9,22-25.29-30; 13,44-52; 14,1-6; 17,13-15; 18,5-6.16-17.28; 21,13; 23, 11.28.30-31). Furthermore, they testified to the resurrection of the dead (24,21;25,29;26,6-8;28,20) as well as to repentance (26,20-21). Their faith in Jesus meant righteousness, chastity, judgment (24,25). It consisted in a turning from darkness to the light, from Satan's dominion to God in order to receive forgiveness and to share in the inheritance, and in revealing this change of heart (μετάνοια) by deeds (26,17-18.20).

Since endurance of indignity for the sake of the name of Jesus made Jesus' disciples worthy of him, suffering was cause for rejoicing (5,14) rather than for disturbance of soul (cf 9,15). Like Jesus, his followers felt that they have to obey God rather than men, even if this obedience meant their death (5,29-33;20,22-24;21,12-14;23,1;24,16 - clear conscience; see also 26,19;27,24 - ordinance).

The external human reason for the suffering of Jesus' followers was, according to the author, the incredulity of the Jews, who refused to "see with their eyes, hear with their ears" (28,26-28). In response to this incredulity the Christians went to the gentiles (18.6;28,25-28) and intended to bring Jesus' blood (5.28) as well as that of Jews upon the Jews themselves (18.6).

At the same time it must be admitted that it was natural that the Jews could not believe Jesus' followers. Their behaviour and actions went contrary to human religious customs, that were holy in the eyes of faithful Jews. So the disciples of Jesus were accused of using blasphemous language against the law and the temple, and of trying to alter the customs that Moses handed down to them (6,13-14; cf 7,52-54; 10,1-11,18; 13,44-47.50-52; 18,13; 20,19; 21,20-26;21, 28.36;22,21-24;23,1-5.12-22;24,1-9; 25,8;28,17-20).

Thus the reason why Christians must suffer and die seems to be the same as it was in Jesus' case: faithfulness to the mission given by God even at the risk of life.

Acts 7,41-43 suggests that the early Christians shared with Amos the tradition (Am 5,25-27) that Israel did not offer any sacrifice to Yahweh during the forty years in the wilderness. They had the tent of testimony but without sacrifice to Yahweh. The only sacrifice that they offered, was to idols which Israelites seemingly liked to do. And the reason for this was, according to the Acts of Apostles, that it gave them satisfaction to do something of their own (ἔργον includes θυσία cf.14,78) and by presenting it to the gods they gain, so they thought, equality with them. But this was displeasing to Yahweh; for having everything, he wanted nothing from them (7,24-25) but only to give. Here we have the most serious argument against sacrifice directed onlyʼ to God and not to men. For the God of Israel wants to give to men, and if sacrifice makes any sense it must be oriented to men.

(3) *The Last Supper - Eucharistic celebration*

In Jerusalem the believers went to the Temple daily to pray, but to break bread they met in private houses (2,42.46). At Troas on a Saturday night Paul himself broke the bread and ate together with the community. Before and after the breaking of bread, Paul addressed them (20,7.11; cf 1 Cor 16,2). A similar ceremony is described in 27,35. At sea, sailing toward Rome, Paul encouraged the sailors to eat something assuring them that they would be not lost in the storm. Having said this, Paul took bread, gave thanks to God in front of them all, broke it and began to eat. Then the others took food. The verb, κλάω (break), is the same as that used in 2,42.46;20,7.11; 1 Cor 10,16; Mk 14,22; Lk 22,16; Mt 26,26. But while the others took *food* (τροφή), the bread taken by Paul was ἄρτος, as in 20,7.11, and 1 Cor 16,2. Paul's eating is expressed by ἐσθίω, (Mt 28.26; Acts 27,35), but the sailors, by προσλαμβάνω. The same distinction is found also in 2,46. Thus "breaking bread" and "taking food" appear as two different actions. Moreover the remark, that Paul gave thanks to God in front of them all (εὐχαρίστησεν τῷ Θεῷ : 27,35), further suggests that the author of the Acts of Apostles was thinking of the same breaking of bread in 27,35 as in 2,42.46 and 20,7. If this is true, 27,35 will be the first case recorded of breaking bread privately in the midst of a non-believing community.

The religious significance of the breaking of bread in the Acts of the Apostles can perhaps be detected also in the context of three other religious activities in midst of which it is mentioned viz., in the teaching of the apostles, κοινωνία and in prayers. The term κοινωνία of 2,42 is a "hapax legomenon" in the Acts of the Apostles. Without adverbial use it occurs in Heb 13,16 together with εὐποιία, and is called explicitly the θυσία of Jesus' followers. In Acts 2,42 it means rather community life, i.e. living not individually but together socially. The expression of this communion with one another (i.e. sharing and doing everything in common), the result of the apostolic teaching, is the breaking of bread. Consequently the only possible sacrificial meaning of the breaking of bread in the Acts of the Apostles would be that of

46

holding and sharing everything in common. Such sharing is witnessed by the New Testament books: in material good (Rom 12,13;15,26; Gal 6,6; Phil 4,15; 2 Cor 9,13), in spiritual goods (1 Cor 1,9) in the gospel (Phil 1,5) of Jesus, as well as in his passion (Phil 3,10; 1 Pet 4,13) and in his body and blood (1 Cor 10,16; cf Heb 2,14); with Jesus in the Holy Spirit (1 Cor 13,13) and with his Father (I Jn 1,6); by living in fellowship with everyone (Gal 2,9; 1 Jn 1,3;1,7; Phm 6) but without sharing in the misdeeds of others (2 Cor 6,14; 1 Tim 5,22;2 Jn 11).

5) *Theology of Sacrifice in the Pauline Writings.*

(1) *Jesus' life and death*

The question why Jesus had to suffer and die takes a new turn in the Pauline writings and its treatment there forecasts its final solution.

In the earliest writings, in the first letter to the Thessalonians, the anger (ὀργή) plays already a considerable role. Jesus raised from the dead will come from heaven to save men from the anger to come (1 Th 1,10), which will come upon all who displease Him (1 Th 2,15.16). Through Jesus Christ who died for them the believers are destined not for wrath but for salvation (1 Th 5,9). Here is the first instance in the New Testament writings where Jesus' death had been connected with the idea of salvation from the wrath of God. The idea will be further developed in the letter to the Romans.[17]

Paul solemnly forewarns the Thessalonians that their concern should be to please (ἀρέσκω) God (1 Th 2,4;4,1) and not to disregard Him, for God is an avenger (ἔκδικος :1 Th 4,6). Unlike the God of the Synoptics who does not appear as angry, Paul's God is an angry avenger who punishes all who disregard Him. On the ground of such a notion of God it is easy to understand that for Paul the notion of expiation, as

47

well as that of the sacrifice, will be of more importance than for the previous writings of the New Testament.

The idea of a punishing and avenging God, so familiar from the Old Testament, is further stressed in the second letter to the Thessalonians. Jesus himself will inflict vengeance and eternal punishment upon those who do not acknowledge God and refuse to accept the gospel (2 Th 1,8-9). Those who are chosen from the beginning to be saved will endure persecution and suffering in order to manifest that the judgment of God is just. Nevertheless all those who afflict the elected of God will repay (ἀνταποδίδωμι) through their own affliction (2 Th 1,6). Thus suffering is inflicted to satisfy the righteousness of God. Since God restricts vengeance to Himself (2 Th 1,5:cf Rom 12,20), Christians should themselves refrain from repaying evil for evil (1 Th 5,14).

God's justice, as the reason for Christ's suffering and death, keeps returning in the later Pauline letters.

In the letter to the Galatians the reason for Christ's death is the justification of men. Were justification possible through the Law, says Paul, then Christ would have died to no purpose (Gal 2,21). He gave himself up for men's sin to deliver them from the present evil age (1,4). The death of Jesus, which made the Law ineffective, revealed also the love of the Son of God, for he gave himself up for Paul (2,20). Thus justice, love and death are systematically connected for the first time in the letter to the Galatians. In order to justify Paul, Jesus died, because he loved Paul. This personal experience of Jesus' love for Paul will be extended as the universal reason for Jesus' death. In the letter to the Galatians, however, it is ultimately not the love but the justification of men that demanded Jesus' suffering and death as its necessary condition. Since Jesus wanted to redeem all who are under Law, he had to be born subject to the Law (Gal 4,5). Now the Law curses everyone who does not persevere in everything

48

that is written in the Law (cf Deut 27,26). Therefore Jesus himself had to become a curse for us(3,13: κατάρα; cf ἁμαρτία of 2 Cor 5,2 and ἐν ὁμοιώματι σαρκὸς ἁμαρτίας of Rom 8,3) and made himself responsible for the curse. Now the Scripture says that the cursed must hang on the tree (3,13; cf Deut 21,23); thus Christ had to die on the tree of the cross. In the letter to the Galatians Jesus had to die to expiate the curse of the Law. But in Col 2,14-15 Paul adds also that Jesus had to disarm cosmic powers in order to be able to nail the decree of the Law to the cross. In brief, Jesus had to suffer and die because he identified himself with men condemned by the Law to death.

This mysterious identification of Jesus with men on the one hand, and on the other, the mysterious identification of men with Christ (cf 2,20: once man is crucified with Christ, he lives no longer but in Christ), seem to provide Paul with the most fundamental principle for solving theological problems. The result of this identification of Jesus with men is that the blessing of Abraham, held back because of sin, will be available for the Jews first and then for the Gentiles in order that all who believe may receive the promise of the Holy Spirit (3,13-14). The reception of this promise comes about, however, not by observing the law but by believing in Jesus; for the promise first given to Abraham was also based on faith and not on the Law, which, given only after 430 years (but cf Acts 7,6), could not invalidate an earlier promise. The purpose of the Law was to reveal transgressions (3,19) and to serve as a custodian until Jesus came (3,24). It helped to consign everything to sin, so that promise might be given only to those who have faith in Jesus Christ. Now in Paul's argument there is a weakness which he does not seem to have noticed. First, how could the Law merely reveal transgressions committed before the Law? Were the Jews before the Law not free to follow the voice of their conscience, like the pagans (cf

Rom 1,18-32)? The only transgression they could commit was a sort of incredulity in respect to the promises of God. Secondly, how could these transgressions withhold the promises of God, if these were promised by God unilaterally? Paul is not considering this. The only point he is making is that Law was supposed to reveal that the promises of God are real promises. Since the Jews could not stay faithful to the Law no one could consider the promise as some sort of God's payment of a debt for Israel faithfulness. Man is left in sin just to show that God's love for men is absolutely free and it is not based upon man's goodness and faithful keeping of the Law.

After having received the free grace of God, there is no distinction between Greek and Jew, free and slave. All are one in Christ, whom they put on like a garment, the symbol of social rank and unity (3,27-28). This is also the meaning of being baptized into Christ (3,27). Once one belongs to Christ he must be crucified to the flesh with its passions and its desires (5,24). On the basis of this unity through the Cross of Jesus by which he was crucified to the world, Jesus' followers also are to be crucified to the world and the world to them. And this is exactly the new creation, separated from the old creation (cf 5,15-25), and having its own Law and rules, viz., those of Christ (6,2).

Interestingly enough, the letter to the Philippians does not go beyond the synoptic theology concerning the reason of Jesus' death. Jesus' death is seen exclusively as obedience to the Father. Jesus humbled himself and became obedient unto death even death on the cross (2,8). But the reason, why had he to be obedient unto death, is not mentioned in the letter. If the theology about the meaning of Jesus' death were a criterion for determining the time of composition of a Pauline Writing, the letter to the Philippians would certainly be considered the first among Pauline Writings.

In the first letter to the Corinthians the why of Christ's suffering is seen as the secret and hidden wisdom of God (2,7-

8). God has chosen the foolish, the weak and the lowly to reveal that God's weakness is stronger than human strength, so that no human being may boast in the presence of God (1,13-31; cf 3,18-22). In other words the meaning of Christ's suffering can be conceived also as a way to humble man through the foolishness of the cross.

As a theological reason for the suffering of Christ, besides that of the folly of the cross, the idea of judgement, known already from the letters to the Thessalonians, is presented. Whereas God judges those outside the Church, the faithful will judge those who are within it (1 Cor 5,12-13) by separating them from the community. But not as the letter to the Thessalonians declares, Christ will not judge in the proper sense of the word, but rather disclose the work of each by the test of fire (1 Cor 3,13-15; 4,5). Each will receive good or evil according to what he has done in this body (2 Cor 5,10).

Sin, however, is for Paul much more than something that deserves punishment and an evil fate. It is something which brings an enmity that must be reconciled (καταλλάσσω). Not as in 1 Th 4,6; Rom 5,9, the anger of God is not mentioned in 2 Cor 5,18-21. It is not God who is going to be reconciled, but rather He is the one who reconciles the world to Himself in Christ and through Christ. The enmity is placed in the sinful world, and God, not man, brings about reconciliation. For it is He and not man who will provide the sin offering (ἁμαρτία), an offering which might correspond to the ḥaṭṭāʾt (sin offering) of the Old Testament offered for the expiation of the sin of Israel. From the fact, however that here it is God who reconciles the world to Himself, it cannot be argued that for Paul expiation was not to be made to God. The point Paul is making is that God did reconcile the world with Himself by offering an expiatory sin sacrifice (for our sake He made him to be a sin-offering: 2 Cor 5,21) so that man might become in Christ the justice of God (2 Cor 5,21). On account of Christ, God will not take account

51

(λογιζόμενος) of the trespasses of men against men (2 Cor 5,19).

Sin as offense against God, who is to be propitiated is implicit in 2 Cor 2,14-15 (cf the idea of the faithful as the aroma of Christ) and explicit in Rom 1,18-19 5.9 according to which man is saved from the anger of God by Jesus' blood (cf Col 3,5).

The word of reconciliation is now entrusted to Paul (2 Cor 5,20), so that he may proclaim that with Jesus the acceptable time has become a reality (cf εὐπρόσδεκτος :2 Cor 6,2c). Thus Christ's suffering seems to be some sort of ransom (τιμή : 1 Cor 6,20;7,23) by which the faithful had been bought, redeemed and freed from the slavery of immorality (1 Cor 6,20) and of other men (1 Cor 7,23) and brought back to God, making him "slave of Christ" i.e. man who is not his own any longer, but belongs to God (1 Cor 6,19). Paul does not say to whom this price was to be paid. His concern is much more the consequences of such a redemption viz., the faithful becomes a member of Christ (1 Cor 6,15-20) and "Christ's incense to God" (2 Cor 2,14-16; cf Col 2,15). The members of Christ will be partners in his triumph by spreading the knowledge of God like a sweet smell everywhere. Paul is here comparing them to the incense offered to Rome after military victories. Like the fragrance of incense that pleases man by presenting a more sublime atmosphere of a new life, so the followers of Christ will please God by the fragrance (εὐωδία) of their new life.   The metaphor of the sacrificial incense suggests the synoptic idea that God is appeased by Christ and He is not angry any more. Jesus died for all that all men should live no longer for themselves but for him who died and was raised to life for them (2 Cor 5,14-15), so that all men might become new creation (2 Cor 5,17) in a new atmosphere of life that was pleasing to God.

Christ died, therefore, for all men (2 Cor 5,15;1 Cor 8,11;1 Cor 11,24) and for their sins (1 Cor 15,4) because he loved men (ἀγάπη τοῦ Χριστοῦ 2 Cor 5,15) as the Father did (2, Cor 13,13). In the letters to the Corinthians the love of God as reason for Jesus' suffering is not as explicit as it is in the letter to the Romans. Jesus' love is connected with God's holiness and justice, and suffering seems to be a necessary condition for actualisation of God's love towards men. He cannot be reconciled with them except through Jesus' death for men. In the letter to the Romans, however, the ultimate reason for Jesus' suffering and death is the visible manifestation of the infinite love of God towards men (cf Rom 5,7-8;8,32).

The letter to the Romans is perhaps the most explicit theological treatise of Paul on the question of why Jesus had to die. The reason for Jesus' death was fundamentally to manifest God's universal mercy by satisfying His justice as well as by expiating His just wrath towards the whole world. Since all have sinned, God's justice demanded that He bring retribution upon men without distinction. Indeed, in the letter to the Romans, the justice and the anger of God seem to be more fundamental than in any other of Paul's letters. The main thesis of the letter is that God's salvation is absolutely free and no one, either Jew or Pagan can claim that he does not need the mercy of God (1,16-3,31).

In order to put everyone under the power of grace, Paul places everyone under the Law of sin (cf 11,32). He thinks that the more universally and more deeply he can show to his readers the righteousness of the universal wrath of God, the more he can demonstrate the universal gratuity of God's mercy. God gave men up justly to their lusts since they did not honor God (1,18-32). This judgment rightly falls upon everyone, since all, as the Scripture says, have turned away from God and all have done wrong (3,12). The gospel reveals the righteousness of God as well as His wrath (1,17-18).

Now in order to manifest not only His righteousness but His grace as well, He offered redemption (ἀπολύτρωσις) in Jesus who was put forward through God as expiation (ἱλαστήριον) by his blood, to be accepted by men in faith (3,21-26). Here however, the expiation is needed not on account of God's anger, but of His justice. Whereas in Rom 5,9 reconciliation is demanded because of God's wrath, man is saved from the anger of God by Jesus' blood (5,9), and has received reconciliation (5,11). In order that the just requirement of the law might be fulfiled and that not man's, but sin's condemnation might be complete (8,31), God sent His son.

It seems that the letter to the Romans brings forward very explicitly the idea that the reason of Jesus' death was the propitiation of an angry God by the blood of His innocent Son. Since this does not occur in previous New Testament writings, there must have been a special reason, for it, inspired particularly by the Roman community.

The fact that the gospel was moving from the Jews to the pagans was considered by many an indication that the Jews were unfaithful and sinners, whereas the pagans were religious and God-serving people. To avert this Paul showed that pagans and Jews were both sinners, and in this regard there was no distinction. The purpose of Jesus' life and obedience was to confirm the truth of the promises made by God to the Jews, and to allow the Gentiles to glorify God for His mercy towards them (15,8-9). To demonstrate God's mercy towards the pagans, Paul could not use the simple synoptic solution. The "because it was written" had to be given a further theological explication. Now the idea of the expiation of an angry God by innocent blood was certainly not unfamiliar to the Romans. They knew about angry gods who asked for placation by expiatory sacrifice. Moreover the idea could have been prompted in Paul by the Jews' rejection of the gospel, which could have frustrated the Pauline missionaries and made them angry. These events of the new missionary activities could have helped to connect Jesus' death with the idea of expiation and expiatory sacrifices. Jesus had to be delivered to death for the misdeeds of men

54

and so through him men obtained access to grace. As sin brought death as its wages (6,23) so Christ's reconciliation brought life and righteousness (5,21), because God's anger, which kills (5,12ff), was removed. By Jesus' death man was justified and raised to new life. In the letter to the Romans there is, however, another idea which was not so familiar to Paul's readers. Jesus' death was not only the expiation of an angry God. It was also the manifestation of God's gratuitous and infinite love towards men. It is well known that even for a good man hardly anyone would die. But Christ died for men who were sinners. Thus he revealed how much God loved men (5,7-8), for by not sparing His son He indicated that He was ready to give men everything (8,32).

The different reasons for the death of Jesus are brought together in synthesis by the idea of the love of God. The reason for Jesus' death is not just the justice of a revenging God but God's infinite love towards all, even sinners and enemies. The death manifests the power of sin as well as the power of God (5,12-21).

Finally there is another new reason for the death of Jesus in the letter to the Romans. This reason is not taken from the religious but from the juridical Roman life. Jesus died, says Paul, in order to free men from an old written code (παλαιότητι γράμματος : 7,6). Since law is binding on a person only during his life time (7,1) so after Jesus' death the law lost its binding force on Jesus and on all who are incorporated into his death by baptism. Through the body of Christ the believer died to the law, so that discharged from the bonds of law, being dead to the law which held men captive, they can serve now in the new life of the spirit (7,4-6).

The death of Christ meant the end of the Old Testament, the end of life according to the flesh (κατά σάρκα) and the beginning of a new order according to the spirit (κατά πνεῦμα). Therefore Jesus' death was necessary in order to

55

reveal the complete newness, the complete independence of the new from the old. In Jesus' death God revealed His willingness to establish a new order which, opposed to the old world of futility and decay, will be a world of triumph and abundance; for God will not refuse men anything He can give them (cf 8,32), and nothing can separate men from God (8,39). In Jesus' death God has shown His retribution at work as well as the wealth of His mercy (9,22-23).

The theology of the letter to the Romans is resumed in the letter to the Colossians. In God there is no partiality. For the wicked deeds of men the anger of God will not fail (3,5). He will repay all wrongdoers. Only the believer will receive the inheritance, since in the beloved Son of the Father he will have redemption (ἀπολύτρωσις) of sin (1,13-14). Through Jesus God reconciled all things to Himself making peace by the blood of the cross (1,20). The blood as the means of reconciliation purifies as well as unites and brings peace to all. Thus by his death in his body of flesh Jesus can present the believer as holy, blameless and irreproachable to God. This offering-function of Christ as well as the purifying power of his blood will be further developed in the letter to the Hebrews.

In Jesus' blood as the means of redemption and of witness to the real value of Christ's work, Paul found an argument to defeat and cast into disrepute the false gnostic teaching of some Colossians, who put forward some special gnostic knowledge as the essence of Christianity. It was not by some doctrine says Paul, but by his cross, that Jesus disarmed the principalities, the elemental spirits of the world (2,8-23). Christ and with him all the faithful died not only to the power of the Law, but also to the power of any elemental cosmic spirits as well as to the force of any human teaching or precept. Thus the synoptic theology about the uncompromising authenticity of the Christian is confirmed in Paul by the idea of death as liberation from any obligation belonging to this world (2,21-3,5). The theme of the letter to the Romans is present in the letter to the Ephesians as well. The Ephesians have received redemption in Jesus through his blood. And this redemption means the remission of sins (1,7). Jesus reconciled men to God through the cross (2,14-22) and thus they have access to the Father (2,18). On account of their transgressions and sins men became children of wrath, but now they have been brought to life with Christ, raised up with him and given a place in heaven with him (2,5-7). In all this God's mercy and great love towards the sinner has been manifested. Consequently the purpose of Christ's life and his death according to the letter to the Ephesians, was to show and manifest the great riches of God's grace and kindness. Since Christ realized this revealing function by manifesting God's love and kindness towards men, he could really become a flagrant offering, a sacrifice to God. By accepting this revelation of God's love towards men as his life-function, he became God's love towards men (5,2). To manifest God's love of men, he became the incarnation of God's love toward men.

The Pastoral letters could not go beyond this profound theology of the letter to the Ephesians. I Tim 6,13 reflects the synoptic theology.

From the context it becomes clear that the confession Jesus made before Pontius Pilate expressed his obedience to the Father in keeping His commandments without fault (1 Tim 6,14). In witness to this he gave himself as a ransom (ἀντίλυτρον) for all (1 Tim 2,6). Tit 2,11 reaffirms the theology of the Ephesians: the grace of God appeared in Jesus Christ for the salvation of men. Jesus gave up himself for men to redeem them from iniquity by purifying them and making them his very own people (2,11-14). Jesus is the goodness and the loving kindness of God (3,4), through whom men are

saved and justified by the cleansing water of regeneration and
the renewal of the Holy Spirit. And Paul rightly insists on
this, because this is true (cf 3,8).

(2) *The life and death of Jesus' followers*

The life of Jesus' followers, according to the first letter to
the Thessalonians, is characterized by two features: first,
faithfulness and obedience to their mission, viz., by proclaiming the Good News to everyone, pagans and gentiles alike,
even if they are persecuted for this (1 Th 2,2-16); and secondly, holiness of life that avoids every immorality, practises
charity, works with one's own hands, and does not repay evil
by evil. This latter should be left to God (1 Th 4,3-8;5,14-28).

The suffering of the believers comes from persecution by
their own countrymen, who try to hinder them from the
teaching to the pagans. They killed the prophets and Jesus, so
they persecute his followers too. Thus they are making up the
full measure of their guilt (1 Th 2,14-16). The faithful,
however, are to please and obey not men but God (1 Th 2,4).
They should never suppress the spirit, but find the will of God
(1 Th 5,19-22).

Consequently the style and way of life of Jesus' followers is
very similar to that of Jesus described by the Synoptics.
Therefore, when Paul applies to such a life, the term "sacrifice", it cannot mean but two things: an obedience to God
instead of men, that accepts human contempt and persecution; and secondly, a pure life of charity dedicated to others;
or in brief, a life of faith, charity and hope (1 Th 1,3).

The second letter to the Thessalonians adds a third feature.
Suffering persecution reveals that God's judgments are just (2
Th 1,4-5). Suffering is a sign of election, since God will reward
all who are suffering now for the sake of kingdom. God is just
in repaying with injury all who do not acknowledge Him, but
He is also just in rewarding those who are afflicted. Suffering

as a revelation of God's justice in the life of Jesus' followers anticipates the idea that is the theme of the letter to the Romans, viz., that Jesus' life is the revelation of God's justice. Here in the second letter to the Thessalonians Paul's own life is given as a model and an example to be imitated (τύπον... τό μιμεῖσθαι : 2 Th 3,7.9). Like Paul, Christ's followers should not be idlers and parasites, but toil and work day and night for their living (2 Th 3,8).

In the letter to the Galatians the meaning of the new life in the spirit, as opposed to the life in flesh, is that the believer does not live his own life, but the life of Christ, who lives in his disciples (2,20). The reason that Jesus lives in the spiritual man is that the faithful have been crucified in Christ, who loved man and gave himself up for them (2,20;3,27-28; 5,24; 6,14). Once Christ who gave himself up for man, lives in the spiritual man, the new life cannot have any meaning but this: love of one's neighbor as of oneself (5,14).

Because union with Christ has brought about one's crucifixion, the new way of life (5,24;6,14;cf the verbal form of στοιχέω instead of the ὁδός of the Synoptics) has a rule (κανών) on its own. The way of the spirit and the way of the flesh are utterly incompatible. The desires of flesh war against the spirit. The fruits of the spirit are love, joy, peace, patience, kindness, goodness, faithfulness, gentleness, self-control which are diametrically opposed to the work of the flesh, sc., immorality, impurity, idolatry, enmity, selfishness, anger, party-spirit etc (Gal 5,16-25;cf 1 Cor 6,9-10; 2 Cor 6,4-10; Rom 1,29-31; Eph 4,17-20; 2 Tim 3,11-12;Tit 2,1-5). The new way is the way of eternal life and alien to the way of flesh, the way of death and corruption (6,8).

The theme of opposition between the life of the spirit and the life of the flesh is present also in the letters to the Corinthians. The life of the spirit is a stumbling block to Jews and folly to the Gentiles (1 Cor 1,22). It is the weakness, foolishness of God opposed to the power and wisdom of the

world (1 Cor 1,20-30;3,18-20;4,8-13). The spiritual man
(πνευματικός) knows the mind of God whereas the un-
spiritual (ψυχικός) is incapable of understanding the mind
of Christ (1 Cor 2,14-3,5). The one who is a member of Christ
cannot live and act in the purely human way of life of an
ordinary man (1 Cor 3,1: σαρκικός; κατὰ ἄνθρωπον). For
one is concerned only with the affairs of God (τά τοῦ
Κυρίου) and the other, only with the affairs of the world
(τὰ τοῦ κόσμου: 1Cor 7,34).

While the external and visible differences between the two
ways are manifested in a long list of diverse moral actions (cf
1 Cor 6,9-10; 2 Cor 6,4-10), their internal natures are the
antipodes of one another. The physical man is living being
(ψυχὴ ζῶσα) like the first Adam but visible (τὰ
βλεπόμενα) perishable (τὸ φθαρτόν) mortal (τὸ θνητόν)
and transient (πρόσκαιρα) drawn from the dust. The
spiritual man is, on the contrary, a spiritual being
(πνευματικός) , like Christ, consequently invisible (μὴ
βλεπόμενα) imperishable (τὸ ἄφθαρτον) immortal
(ἀθανασία) permanent (αἰώνιος) made after the image
of man of heaven (cf 1 Cor 15,42-19; 2 Cor 4,18; 2 Cor 5,9).
The two kinds of men are also referred to by Paul respectively
as "those outside" and those "inside"; as (οἱ ἔξω and
οἱ ἔσω: 1 Cor 5,12-13), "the outward" and "the inward
man" (ὁ ἔξω...ἄνθρωπος and ὁ ἔσω... 2 Cor 4,16); as the
old and the new man (ὁ παλαιός ἡμῶν... Rom 6,5;
ὁ καινὸς ἄνθρωπος Eph 2,15) as man according to flesh and
man according to spirit (κατὰ σάρκα and κατὰ πνεῦμα :
Rom 8,5; cf also Rom 2,28-29).

Since the faithful have been bought with a price by Christ,
they belong not to man but to God, and they cannot therefore
live like others. The sin they commit with their body is a
sacrilege against God, because in a certain sense they force
Christ, whose members they are, into sin (cf 1 Cor 6,13-20).
For the same reason they cannot participate in Christ and at

the same time in the table of demons (1 Cor 10,14-21). Behavior such as that provokes the Lord's jealousy (1 Cor 10,24). The faithful's not-belonging to the world, however, does not mean their opposition to the world. They are supposed rather to gain the world's sympathy in order to save it. Like Paul whom the Corinthians are to imitate, as he does Christ, so every one of the faithful should be free from all men in order to make himself the slave of everyone, so as to win as many as he can (1 Cor 9,19). No one should give offense to anyone, to Jews or Greeks or to the Church of God, but try to be helpful to everyone at all times, anxious not for his own advantage but for the advantage of everybody else, so that they may be saved (1 Cor 10,32-33).

As charity is the greatest gift of God, the new code given in 1 Cor 13 makes charity the standard of the new life in the spirit. Since the perfection (τέλειος) of charity will be specially manifested in the time of factions and divisions among the faithful, this is the reason, precisely, why factions in the Church are permitted by God. The genuine among the faithful will be recognized in this way (1 Cor 11,19).

Union with Christ and sharing in his afflictions serve another purpose for by suffering and the experience of their own afflictions the faithful become able to comfort those who are similarly afflicted (2 Cor 1,3-7), and those who share in Christ's suffering share in his comfort and his triumph as well (1 Cor 1,5). Because of this union the Christians are not only the fragrance of Christ (2 Cor 2,15; cf Sir 39,14;24,15) but also the splendor (δόξα) of God, being transformed from one degree of glory to another (2 Cor 3,14-18; cf 1 Cor 15,40-41). Such transformation is also expressed by the term ἐπενδύω which means putting on something new, and by the term καταπίνω, being taken or swallowed like a drink, with its suggestion of sacrificial libation. The consequence is that instead of being far away from the Lord and exiled from

Him, Jesus' followers will walk in the presence of God (2 Cor 5,6-9; notice the notion of walking ἐνδημέω, ἐκδημέω with κατὰ ἄνθρωπον of 1 Cor 3,3 and God's way in the Synoptics). Suffering, sadness, grief in the way of God mean changing for the better (μετάνοια) and leave no regrets, whereas suffering according to the world means death (2 Cor 7,11-12). Taken in this sense μετάνοια suggests that the notion of sacrifice is being applied to the lives of Jesus' followers: sacrifice means μετάνοια.

Since Christ though rich became poor, the faithful should offer service to the saints. God loves the cheerful giver. He will supply and multiply the resources of the believer overwhelmingly. Thus the poverty of the giver becomes the riches of the Church (8,9;9,1-12). Moreover helping the needy and poor is the best sign of Christian authenticity and orthodoxy (cf Gal 2, 9-10).

In the letter to the Romans the meaning of the suffering of Christ's followers is seen in its power of bringing about patience and perseverance, which in turn engender hope, and hope reveals God's love, poured into the heart through the Holy Spirit given to men (5,3-5). The fact of exulting in present suffering shows that the Holy Spirit is given to men, since it is charity that is cause of the hope manifested in suffering. The movement from suffering to the love of God in Rom 5, 2-3 is epistemological rather than ontological. In the mind of Paul it is not suffering which leads man to love of God, but rather suffering manifests and makes known that the love of God has really been given to man. Knowing this, the faithful are to rejoice in suffering as in the sign of the love of God, who suffered for sinful man.

Moreover, suffering is also the necessary condition of the internal transformation, in virtue of which the whole creation is going to be set free from its bondage to decay and futility in order to obtain redemption and conformation to the image (εἰκών) of the Son of God (Rom 8,20-30). Through baptism into the death of Christ the believer walks (περιπατέω) in newness of life (6,3-4). The old self (παλαιὸς ἄνθρωπος) and the sinful body (τὸ σῶμα τῆς ἁμαρτίας) is destroyed (καταργέω: 6,6) so that man no longer lives enslaved to sin under the old written code (παλαιότης γράμματος), but in the new life of the spirit (καινότης : Rom 7,6), having become rather the slave of God and of righteousness (6,18.22). Man freed from the power of sin, which did not allow him to follow God's will (8,5-11), is transformed by the baptismal renewal and can now discover the will of God and know what is acceptable and perfect before God.

Once transformed into the image of the Son, Jesus' followers should not be conformed to the world. This being not-conformed to the world is the new spiritual life, i.e. meaningful (12,1: λογικός; cf 1 Cor 14,19: λόγους τῷ νοΐ) worship and service of God. Once the ritual sacrifices of the Jews and of the pagans (cf Rom 1,9; Hos 6,6) became unacceptable and meaningless after Christ, the new life of the faithful is the only meaningful sacrifice. Sanctified by the Holy Spirit, not only the Jews but also the Gentiles can become an acceptable and holy offering to God (15,16: ἡ προσφορὰ τῶν ἐθνῶν gen obj.). Such a sacrifice is basically genuine love, fulfilment of law (13,8), hatred of evil, contributing to the need of others and never repaying evil for evil. Instead it overcomes evil with good (16,20), and never passes judgment on others (cf 12,3-15,33). Thus Paul and the faithful are instruments in the hand of God, who wants to bring the Gentiles into obedience through the words and deeds of the believers, as signs and through the power of the Holy Spirit (15,15-19). Yet the suffering endured does not deserve to be compared with the glory to be revealed (8,18) and due to the suffering with Christ (8,17).

According to the letter to the Philippians, obedience (2,12; cf 2,4-10) is the sacrifice and offering of faith (gen obj.: faith offers obedience as a sacrifice) in which Paul and his life are poured out as a libation (2,17-18). The faithful who obey without complaining and arguing are blameless, innocent and faultless (ἄμωμος), children of God, like the lamb of Isaiah, symbol of the suffering, obedient servant of God (2,14-17). The adjective ἄμωμος might suggest that Paul had in mind not only the suffering servant of Yahweh, but also the Paschal Lamb (cf its application to Christ: Eph 1,4; Heb 9,14; to the Church: Eph 5,27; and to the Christians: Phil 2,15; Col 1,22)

Once death becomes the condition for resurrection, the loss of all things is unimportant if Christ can be gained so (3,8-11). To gain Christ means a constant reaching out for what lies ahead and straining forward to win the prize (βραβεῖον: its profane use in 1 Cor 9,24;Phil 3,14). Paul's pressing on in order to gain Christ is an example (τύπος) to be imitated (3,17; cf 2 Th 3,9: μιμέομαι). While the enemies of the cross of Christ will perish, Jesus' followers transfigured (μετασχηματίζω) into "copies of Christ's glorious body", will have their homeland in heaven (3,18-21). Alms and gifts given by the Philippians to Paul are "a sweet fragrance", an offering acceptable and pleasing to God (4,17-19), like those of Ex 29,18 and Ez 20,41, burnt during the ordination of the priests.

The letter to the Colossians presents a new reason for the suffering of Jesus' followers: they have to complete what is lacking in Christ's sufferings for the Church (1,24-25). Like Christ who presents the faithful to God, holy and blameless and irreproachable, by his death, so Paul and the Colossians present themselves (1,22.28:παρίστημι and not προσφέρω, since the offerer has a more active role in offering himself than the priest in offering sacrifice) to God by sharing in Christ's sufferings. But sacrifice must be irreproachable before its presentation. So the Colossians are to be free from the empty deceit of human traditions, customs, man-made philosophy based on some elementary spirits (στοιχεῖον) of the world. External ceremonies, such as the new moon, sabbath rites, rules for drinking etc., are just shadows. The reality (σῶμα) is Christ (2,16-19). Merely human teaching, devotion, even mortification are of no use at all (2,21-3,4). The old is to be put off and the new is to be put on (3,9-11).

The originality of the new life and its incompatibility with the old is the real sacrifice, in the sense that it puts to death immorality, idolatry etc (3,5). It serves no man, but God in every man (3,18-24) striving for the fulness of God (2,8-10;4,5) being seasoned with salt, as the sacrifices used to be, in order to please and to attract everyone to Christ (4,5-6). The letter to the Ephesians describes the lives of Jesus' followers in a similar way. The old nature which belóngs to the old manner of life (4,22: προτέραν ἀναστροφήν) and follows the course of the world and the desires of body and the passions of the flesh (2,1-3; cf 5,4.17-20) is to be put off by virtue of Christ's work of reconciliation. One must put on instead the new man, created after the likeness of God's life, which is a life of meekness, love and peace (4,1-3;4,25-32;5,3-6,9). Once Jesus' followers have become light (5,7) and able to understand the will (θέλημα) of the Lord, they must fight evil, armed with truth as a girdle, with righteousness as a breastplate, with the gospel of faith as shoes, with faith as a shield, with salvation as a helmet, and with the word of God as the sword of the Spirit (6,10-17). In his last letter, Paul is more convinced than ever that whoever wants to live an authentic life in Christ will be persecuted, because evil goes from bad to worse. For this cause his blood too will be shed as a libation (2 Tim 4,6 σπένδομαι; Phil 2,17). The sacrifices of shedding his blood is the definitive departure (2, Tim 4,6: ἀνάλυσις i.e. to unloose his tent for departure).

(3) The Last Supper-Eucharistic celebration

Paul is dealing explicitly with the Eucharistic celebration in 1 Cor 11,17-34 and less explicitly in 1 Cor 10,14-21. Since these texts were analysed when we dealt with the use of θυσία and αἷμα here only few remarks will be made. Paul carefully distinguishes the Lord's Supper (1 Cor 11,20: κυριακὸν δεῖπνον) from the private meals of the participants (1 Cor 11,21: ἴδιον δεῖπνον). The latter are to satisfy hunger and should not be the reason for coming together in the assembly of the faithful. Hunger can be satisfied at home just as well. The meaning of the Lord's meal has not this purpose but that of proclaiming the death of the Lord until he comes. The meal is just the occasion of the celebration of the Lord's death. Its symbolic meaning is related not to the meal, but to the death of Christ (1 Cor 11,21-34).

The general atmosphere of Paul's tradition concerning the Lord's Supper is no longer that of the Passover. It is a gathering of the faithful who commemorate Christ by waiting for his coming again. The commemorative repetition is recommended twice: "Do this in memory of me". Therefore it supposes a church where the frequent celebration of breaking bread was practised some time ago. The celebration however does not aim at the remission of sins directly, but at the commemoration of Jesus' death, which includes or supposes the proclamation of his next coming. Jesus' death and resurrection is celebrated therefore under the form of his last farewell-party, which at the same time was the proleptic form of his coming in the eschatological age.

6) *Theology of Sacrifice in the Letter to the Hebrews*

(1) *Jesus' life and death*

The letter written to the Hebrews is perhaps the only book of the New Testament which could be called a manual of the theology of sacrifice. It is so full of cultic-sacrificial impact that it can reasonably be assumed that not only the writer but the readers as well were priests, for whom the idea of sacrifice was a fundamental way of understanding any religious issue. Being priests with sacrificial functions, the original uniqueness of Jesus could not have been demonstrated to them otherwise than by indicating that he was unique, and a priest forever in the most original way. Supposing this, the main thesis, viz., that Jesus is not only High Priest in the proper sense, but that he is so forever, transcending any priesthood ever known, is very understandable.

Interestingly enough, the author sees the function of the High Priest not in discovering the will of God by Urim and Thummim (cf Num 27,21; Ex 28,15-30) or in blessing (like Melchizedek in 7,1) or in attending national ceremonies (2 Chron 19,5-11), but only in offering gifts and sacrifices. The High Priest is seen here essentially as making expiation to God and cleansing men from their sins (e.g. 5,1;7,27;10,12). A possible reason for this is that the author felt that only the sacrificing function can be applied to Jesus in the most eminent way.

Now Jesus is High Priest, because like any High Priest he was called by God (5,4), to act as representative of men in their relation to God (5,1); for their benefit offering gifts and sacrifices. Jesus however is not only High Priest, he is the only efficient and perfect High Priest, because only he could really be in touch with God by entering into Heaven, and could in reality cleanse the consciences of men (10,22;9,14;10,18) by offering to God the most perfect sacrifice, himself (7,27; 9,26.28) and his own blood (7,26-28;10,11-18;9,12), as well as prayers and supplications with cries and tears (5,7). Now such an offering is evidently more valuable than the blood of goats, calves and bulls.

Moreover since he dies no more, no other priesthood or no other priests are needed. Having offered the most perfect sacrifice no further sacrifice is required. Finally since he is in

67

heaven he can constantly intercede for men. After having sacrificed, the function of Jesus in heaven is twofold: saving and interceding (7,25).

The meaning of Jesus' life therefore as it appears in the letter to the Hebrews, is priestly and sacrificial. He made purification for sins (1,3;9,14: καθαρίζω), making expiation (2,17: ἱλάσκομαι) for the sins of the people in the most perfect way, since he himself is without blemish (9,14), holy and not belonging to the community of sinners (7,26). His death redeems (ἀπολύτρωσις) all who are called by God from their transgressions under the first covenant (9,15). By offering himself and making himself a sacrifice, he did away with sin and took upon himself the burden of man's sins (9,28). To do this, however, he needed to shed his blood. The reason for this is that without blood there is no forgiveness, and almost everything is purified by blood (9,22). This religious conviction taken from the Old Testament gives the author a direct theological reason for the necessity of Jesus' shedding his blood. The conviction that there is no purification without blood, supposes sin as an act of taking away something which belongs to God. Now by shedding blood, which manifestly belongs to Him, its restoration to God is symbolized. This idea of pouring out blood as a symbol of referring to God is present also in the notion that there is no covenant without the shedding of blood. By this latter every covenant was protected and sanctioned by God, to whom blood belonged.

For the same reason blood had a uniting and sanctifying power. By shedding his blood, therefore, Jesus not only purified man from his sins, but also sanctified (ἁγιάζω) him (cf 13,12). To achieve this, however, he had to suffer outside the gate, as in the atonement sacrifice of Lev 16,1-34. By this image the author suggests sacrifice as some sort of going forth from the present transitory city to the home which is to come (cf 13,13-14).

When Jesus comes for the second time, he will not deal again with sin, but will save those who are waiting for him. He made satisfaction for sin once for all, but apparently only for those committed under the first covenant. The author seems to limit the value of Jesus' death to the sins committed under the Old covenant but not to those committed in the New (cf 9,15; 6,4-8; 10,26-31).

The purpose of Jesus' death and sacrifice, however, was not just the remission of sins, but also reconciliation with God the Father. Since God did not take pleasure in sacrifices (θυσία⁰), offerings (προσφορά), burnt offerings and sin offerings (ὁλοκαυτώματα... περὶ ἁμαρτίας) Jesus came to do His will (10,8-9). By his obedience he sanctified all once for all (10,10), and saved men from the judgment of an angry God (10,26-31; cf Deut 32,35-36). The God of the letter to the Hebrews is again vengeful. It is fearful thing to fall into the hand of the living God (10,30) who is a consuming fire (12,9).

In addition to remission of sins, reconciliation with God, obedience to God, there is a further reason for Jesus' death. Jesus' death was necessary to inaugurate the new covenant. The idea is known from the letter to the Romans, but here there is a slight difference. A covenant must be ratified with blood (9,17). And the blood of Christ manifests the everlasting faithfulness of God (7,28). It fulfills the function of an oath.

But there is also a truly new reason for Jesus' suffering: sc., solidarity with the suffering mankind. By the grace of God he tasted death for everyone (2,9). Through his sufferings he could become the perfect leader of those who are to be saved (2,10). For by sharing in suffering, the one who sanctifies and those who are sanctified have a common experience and origin, and so can be called brethren (2,11). Jesus had to be made like his brethren in every respect in order to learn mercy and faithfulness. Since he suffered and was tempted, he is able to help those who are tempted (2,18). He can sympathize with weakness of men, since he had been tempted in every respect, except with sinning (4,14). On man's behalf he has gone on as a forerunner (πρόδρομος) to heaven, in order to become a sure and steadfast anchor of hope for all (6,19-20). Bearing the sins of many (9,28), he entered into heaven and appeared in the presence of God on man's behalf (9,24). Finally the meaning of Jesus' death is considered not only in regard to God and to men, but also in regard to the devil. Through his death he overcame the devil, who had the power of death. But Jesus delivered all those who were subject to his slavery (2,14-15) and because of his death he was crowned with glory and honor (2,9).

(2) The life and death of Jesus' followers

Since the blood of Jesus is like a new way into the sanctuary, i.e. into the presence of God, opened up through the curtain of his body, the faithful can enter the Holy of Holies, as did the High Priest, (10,19) and assume priestly functions. Though they are not called priests, as in 1 Pet 2,5,9 and Apoc 1,6;5,10;20,6, they are asked to offer praise to God, i.e. to acknowledge God's name and his benefits, and this is called (θυσία·) sacrifice, as are good deeds of sharing all with others (κοινωνία). The faithful, like Jesus, have to please God by doing His will. By struggling against sin as well as by loving each other, they perform an acceptable ministry (12,28: λατρεύω), that brings about the faith and confidence which characterizes the life of the faithful (3,14;4,-16;10,19-25;10,35;11,4-31). Lack of confidence is a great defect, and cannot escape punishment (2,2).

Suffering and endurance (παιδεία) have an educational purpose for the faithful. It is painful, but it yields the fruit of righteousness for those who are trained by it (10,32-34;12,7-11). The struggle against sin is similar to the shedding of

suffering really consists is not explained by 1 Peter. The author might have intended salvation from the judgment of an angry God. "For if a good man is scarcely saved", he quotes Pr 11,31, "who knows, what the end of the impious sinner will be?" (1 Pet 4,17-18; 2 Pet 2,9-22). The devil prowls around like a roaring lion, seeking some one to devour. Consequently Jesus' followers must strive zealously to be found by Jesus without spot and blemish (2 Pet 3,14). They are to love each other, be subject to the authorities, follow the way of truth (ἡ ὁδὸς τῆς ἀληθείας),   which can indeed be brought into disrepute by false teachers (2 Pet 2,1-2). Keeping themselves unstained by the world, standing firm when trials come, they will receive the crown of life which God promised to those who love Him (Jam 1,12) now without seeing Him (1 Pet 1,8).

(3) *The Last Supper - Eucharistic celebration*

1 Pet 1,2 indicates an interesting purpose for the apostolic calling. The writer feels that he had been chosen and destined not only for sanctification by the Spirit, for obedience to the Father, but also for the sprinkling with the blood of Christ. The trinitarian formula sees the function of the apostle in sprinkling with the blood of Jesus, which, as it appears from the context, means the invitation of men into the New Covenant established in Jesus' blood. The sprinkling of the blood of Jesus may have some relation with the Last Supper, as it is witnessed in the early tradition. In such a case, witnesses to the suffering of Christ are not necessarily eye-witnesses to Jesus' death, but simply those who celebrated the Eucharist with others as a memorial of the Lord's suffering, death and glory (cf 1 Pet 5,1). They are the shepherds who take care of the flock of God,   and who are themselves examples (τύποι) to it. (1 Pet 5,1-3).

8) *The Theology of Sacrifice in the Johannine Writings*

(1) *Jesus' life and death*

The author of the Gospel according to John is aware of the evolution which took place between the life time of Jesus and the theologizing efforts on the part of Jesus' followers to understand why things really happened the way they did. The disciples led by the Holy Spirit came slowly to an understanding, of them, which was not possible for them at the beginning (cf 2,22;14,5.14.22.26;16,1-4.12-15;16,17-19;20,9). In a certain sense, the Gospel according to John brings together all the insights of previous New Testament writings into the meaning of Jesus' life and death in order to systematize them, and to express them in a light proper to the author himself.

Like the Synoptics, John too is convinced that Jesus met his death because he was faithful to his divine vocation and would not conform to the surrounding world of men. The opposition between Jesus and the leaders of his people led necessarily to the point at which Jesus had to witness the truth by his blood (cf 2,13-21;5,10-18.42-47;6,64-66;7,20-24.45-52; 8,44-59; 10,36-39; 12,42-43; 15,18-27; 16,5-11; 19,7.16. 22;18,14.28-37;19,7-16). The new element in John is that Jesus has come to give witness to what he has seen in Heaven (3,31-32; cf 7,14;8,40;16,28), and to communicate it to men as God's own word (3,34;5,31-38;7,16) even if his witness is not accepted (3,33-32;cf 1,11). Jesus' witnessing by his blood is expressed also in 1 Jn 5,6-10 where together with the witness by water and that of the Holy Spirit it is called the witness of God Himself, since He has borne witness in it for His son (1,Jn 5,9).

Thus the intrigues and annoyances existing between Jesus and his opponents received in John a deep theological significance. The actual historical reason of Jesus' death and its

74

theological meaning are not separated any longer. The historical, visible, human sign conveys the transcendentally invisible, divine meaning (faith). For John, Jesus' seemingly intransigent, uncompromising attitude toward the world, which was the cause of his death, is at the same time the manifestation to the world of God's limitless love. The external, historical reason became the symbol of a love, faithful at any cost, at any time. Since in Jesus' life and death not only the fact but also the nature of God's love towards men was revealed, the why of Jesus' life and death is to be found ultimately in the nature of the divine love towards men.

Now the essence of the divine love is understood by John as a boundless self-giving to the one beloved. Just as by reason of His love for His Son, the Father gives everything (3,55), shows everything (5,20;cf 5,26-27: source of life; 6,27;10,17-18: judgment etc.) to the Son, so by reason of his love, in turn, the Son gives himself to the Father. The meaning of Jesus' life and death was indeed as the Synoptics have stated, to fulfil the Scriptures (2,22;5,39-40;19,28.36-37 etc.). The meaning of the Scriptures for Jesus, however, is not some written law, but his Father's will (4,34), the commands given him by the Father (10,18). Obedience to the Father (cf 8,28-29.40;12,48-50;14, 31;15,9-11) is his food, and his life is said to be consummated (19,30), when he has accomplished the work the Father gave to him (17,4). For the same reason he lays down his life. This is his vocation given by the Father and the Father loves him for that same reason (10,15.18; cf 12,49).

Love as an unlimited giving of oneself to the Father includes the power of withdrawing oneself from everything else in order to give oneself completely to God. Self-giving thus involves in itself a semblance of death (cf 12,24-25). For since love is an unlimited self-giving to another, death almost becomes the necessary condition of the realization of the greatest love (cf 15,13). It does indeed manifest who a man is (cf 7,28) and the power that his love has (12,31-32).

Besides these two elements, unlimited self-giving and complete free self-possession, there is a third feature of the divine love revealed in Jesus' life and death. A love which is unlimited and absolutely free is now essentially man-oriented. Its unlimited free self-giving is indeed realized in a self-giving to man. But it is only when God has manifested His love by giving His Son for men that men might have life (3,16;cf 1,12-13; 2,21; 5,29; 6,39-54; 10,10-11; 11,25-26; 15,1-17), that man can really understand in what love consists, viz., in laying down one's life for men (1 Jn 3,16). God's love indeed has been disclosed: He has sent His only Son into the world to bring life and to be the expiation (ἱλασμὸς) for the sins (1 Jn 4,9-10) of the whole world (1 Jn 2,2).

Since life and the remission of sin are connected, Jesus is introduced at the beginning of the gospel as the Lamb of God who takes away the sins of the world. He is a sacrificial, expiatory victim for the remission of sin (1,29.36). The Lamb is a significant symbol for John and includes two things: the idea of the servant of Is 53, who takes on himself the sins of men, and that of the lamb, - the lamb of expiation of Lev 14 as well as that of the Passover Lamb of Ex 12,1 (cf Jn 19,36).

In such a context it is not surprising that, unlike the Synoptics, John's Gospel speaks of the anger of God, as did the Epistles of Paul. Unlike those, however, it appears to represent the divine anger as unapproachable. It falls upon those who will not believe (3,36). While Jesus takes away the sin of disbelief, he does not make it impossible; rather, he reveals its real essence, (cf 3,18-21.36;10.22-29,11,45-47;12,42-43.48: 15,18-27;16,5-11). The two worlds, - one, the world of blood, flesh and the will of men (1,13), the world of this earth and the other, coming from above, the world of the Spirit and of God Himself (1,13,3.3-8,31:8.23)-are incompatible. For this reason, 1 Jn, like the letter to the Hebrews, doubts that the propitiation offered by Jesus is without limits. There is one sin that is deadly, for which John suggests no prayer (5,16-17). The reason for this, in turn, is found in the freedom that is a necessary condition for love. Jesus did come, indeed, to save the world, not to condemn it (12,46-47); but those who do not believe are condemned already (3,18). He died to gather together the scattered children of God (11,52) only.

Similarly, the victory of the Lamb of the book of Revelation does not entail the impossibility of his being rejected. The Lamb, as the Lord of History, opens the seals of the different epochs (5,6;22,9). He has freed men from sin by his blood, and has made a kingdom of priests of God, i.e. a new covenant with men (1,5). By his blood he has ransomed for God men from every tribe and nation and has made of them a kingdom (5,9), a people who have washed their robes white in his blood (7,13). Thus the Lamb has manifested his love for men (1,5). The Lamb, however, who loves, knows also wrath, which all his enemies fear (6,16; cf 15,7.14;16,1;19,15) for he has come to repay everyone according to what he deserves (22,12).

(2) *The life and death of Jesus' followers*

The followers of Jesus are born not from blood, nor from the will of men, but from God himself (1,13). They will have eternal life through faith (3,15-16). Their good deeds have the purpose of revealing that they were done really in God, and thus of manifesting the presence of God, acting in them. As new creatures (4,23-24), they receive from Jesus new life, which like a spring inside men wells up to eternal life (4,4-14;7,37-38). Like Jesus, they must lose their life in order to keep it (12,24), and love each other by giving up life for each other as a sign of the greatest love (15,12). Since divine love, as self-giving, is essentially man-oriented, the double commandment of Mark and Matthew (12,29-21;22,37-39) can be resumed in the Johannine theology by one: love one another (1 Jn 2,7-10;3,11.16-17). According to Rev 2,10, suffering is the trial by which faith is tested and receives the crown of life.

(3) The Last Supper-Eucharistic celebration

The multiplication of wine (2,1-11), followed by the multiplication of bread (6,1-15), is described by John in the light of the Eucharistic celebration. The real, eternal life is to eat Jesus' flesh and drink his blood (6,53-56). All who eat him, will have life because of him (6,57), for he is the bread of God come down from heaven to give life to the world (6,33-35.48-51.57-58). Eating Jesus' flesh and drinking his blood is to have eternal life, because it includes the presence of Jesus and his Father (6,56-57), from whom Jesus draws his own life.

The language of the Eucharistic celebration could very well indeed appear "intolerable" (cf 6,60). The identification of Jesus with the bread and wine is so close that the properties of one are predicated of the other. Once the love of God, as the only way of life for Jesus, was to be seen in his self-giving, it was not too difficult to see a symbolic relationship between Jesus and the bread and wine which he gave at the Last Supper to his disciples as a memorial of himself. This self-giving love is the evident milieu of the Last Supper in the Johannine tradition; he showed them that his love was indeed unlimited (13,1: εἰς τέλος ; 13,2-16; cf 13,34-35;14,2-3.18-21.31;15,1-17;16,20-33;17,1-26).

After the victory of the Lamb in the book of Revelation, his faithful followers are invited as brides (22,9) to the marriage supper prepared by the Lamb (19,9), where the glory of God is the light and the Lamb is the lamp. The infinite love, proleptically described at the last Supper will be definitively realized at the marriage banquet of the Lamb.

78

2. The Prehistory of the Sacrificial Interpretation of Jesus' Achievement

After having examined the theology of sacrifice found in the writings of the N.T., we must now analyse their sources. A source criticism of the New Testament writings includes not only the immediate sources, i.e. the life of the post-paschal community before the Gospels but also the mediate sources, viz., the surrounding cultures with their twofold stream of influences: the Canaanitic, Iranian and Egyptian on the one hand, and the Hellenistic Greek, together with the Latin Roman religious civilization on the other.

The present study will be limited to the immediate sources sc., to the life of the post-paschal community before the gospels.[18]

Now in dealing with the life of the post-paschal community in its pre-literary stage we have to distinguish two questions: one is that of the Last Supper and its sacrificial interpretation, and the other, that of the history of the sacrificial

interpretation of Jesus' achievement itself. We will begin with
the prehistory of the Eucharistic words of the Last Supper.

A. *THE PREHISTORY OF THE LAST SUPPER'S SACRIFICIAL INTERPRETATION*

A theological understanding of the Last Supper as a sacrificial event could have arisen from its relation either to Jesus'
death or to the Jewish Passover, or finally to a sacrificial meal
known among the members of Qumran community.

1) *The Eucharistic Words in Their Relation to Jesus' Death*

The most obvious sacrificial interpretation of the Last
Supper would result from its direct relationship with the
sacrifice of the Cross. Indeed the verb "pouring out" in all
three instances (Mt 26,28; Mk 14,23; Lk 22,20) is in the
future tense, indicating that Jesus' blood will be poured out
very soon. This seemed to be confirmed by the tradition of
Paul, in which the relationship of the pouring out of blood
with Jesus' death on Calvary is no longer considered explicitly. Unlike the Synoptic tradition, Paul's tradition directly suggests some sort of commemoration of the past rather
than a future event. Paul does not in fact mention the
pouring out of the blood.

In the Synoptic context the Last Supper seems to be given
as an interpretation of Jesus' death and its meaning. Mark
and Matthew seem to extoll the blood of Jesus as blood of the
covenant and thus to remind us of Ex 24,8, whereas Luke and
Paul stress also the newness of the covenant by suggesting Jer
31,31. The common interpretation of the Synoptics is nevertheless the same: Jesus is going to suffer and die for others,
which by Matthew is understood to be for the sins of others.

The suffering of the just man, interpreted as suffering for

the sins of others, was known to Isaias (53 ch.). While the criminal was asked to pray before his execution: "May my death atone for all my sins" (Leviticus rabba 20,7), the death of the just made atonement for others. The Qumran community, for example, considered not only their work and suffering as making atonement for the land, but also - above all, in the case of the hasīdīm martyred under Antiochus, - as a propitiation that would avert God's wrath from the nation.[19] In the somewhat earlier document of Dan 7,25-26, also the propitiatory aspect is implicit.

The Last Supper's relation to the Cross is further suggested by the terms "body" and "blood".[20] The Greek ἐστιν is not used in the Aramaic language, so the meaning might be any kind of relation: real as well as symbolic. J. Dupont suggests that real relationship can be deduced from the given sacrificial context, which supposes a real communion with the victim. If the Last Supper is a real sacrifice, the bread and wine must have a real and not only a symbolic relationship with Christ's body and blood.[21]

Dupont supposes that the Last Supper has indeed a real sacrificial context. The real question is, however, in what does the sacrificial context consist?

The most feasible solution seems to be that the "is" could have been understood by the early Christians in the sense of epiphanic symbols, in which God became present to his people. Now since the symbol contained the symbolized reality and the symbol, according to their understanding of it, received all its value precisely from the real presence of the symbolized reality, the body and blood of Jesus which was going to be sacrificed on the cross had to be present in the bread and wine, and would thus give a sacrificial character to the Last Supper.[22]

A serious objection to this solution is how a sacrifice which is not yet accomplished could be present in the Last Supper. The immediate future of pouring the blood is imminent but not present.

But the fundamental question is whether Jesus' death was seen as "sacrifice". When and in what sense?

2) *The Eucharistic Words in Their Relation to Passover*

A much easier answer to our question would be the one which contends that the Last Supper was conceived as a sacrifice by the early Christians because they thought of it as a Passover meal in accordance with the Old Testament. Indeed, there is a Jewish tradition which called the Passover a sacrifice (Ex 12,25-27:*zabah;* Deut 16,2.5.6: *asa zabah* communion sacrifice) Flavius Joseph testifies in this sense.[23] According to Mekhilta's commentary the blood of the lamb had a redemptive value.[24] It is also true that the New Testament writers link the Last Supper with the Passover,[25] but it is questionable whether the early Christians from the beginning saw the Last Supper as a sacrifice, since they were not of the rabbinical school.

The relationship of the Last Supper with the Passover ceremony involves the problem of the time when Jesus and his disciples actually celebrated the Last Supper. According to Mark and Matthew, it was on the Preparation day of the Passover, Nisa 15. According to John it took place on the day before the Preparation day, and Jesus died on the Preparation day itself, when the Jews took the passover meal (cf Jn 13,1, with 13,29;18,28 and 19,14.31). John has, indeed, a special interest in showing that Jesus was the real Paschal Lamb (19,36). Now, if, according to John, Jesus and his disciples did not celebrate on the Preparation day, their meal could not have been the Passover, but just a religious meal. A. Jaubert [26] tried to solve this question by introducing two different calendars. Indeed the Qumran community had a solar calendar agreeing with the Sadducean priestly tradition, which differed from the Pharisean calendar, based on a moon-solar system, that was used in Jerusalem. Now according to the Qumran calendar the Passover was celebrated always on the same day, so that it could have been celebrated legally on Tuesday evening. It seems therefore according to Jaubert that the Synoptics followed this calendar now known from the Qumran discoveries, whereas John followed the official calendar observed in Jerusalem. In this view the difficulties of the two sessions of the Sanhedrin can be solved more easily, since there is more time given for the trial of Jesus. The solution, nevertheless, raises more difficulties than it solves, and it has not been accepted generally[27]

3) *The Eucharistic Words in Their Relation to Zikkārôn, Ḥaburah and to Qumran Community's Meal*

According to others[28] the Last Supper was rather a form of *Zikkārôn,* a memorial meal, similar to the one described in Ex 12,14ff. In the view of F. L. Leenhardt, the remembrance of the past was, according to the Hittite customs, a condition for any covenant, insofar as recalling the past situation which conditioned the covenant, it was supposed to guarantee and keep the covenant alive for the time to come. Thus the meal was a certain participation in the permanent actualization of the covenant and, more concretely, in the liberation brought about by Yahweh.

Again, according to some others, the Last Supper was rather a confraternity meal, *Ḥaburah.* The one presiding at the meal gave the blessing of the bread while the others answered "Amen". For the wine any individual might give a personal blessing, but at the end the president gave a final benediction of the cup with a longer prayer, giving thanks for creation, the exodus, the covenant; meanwhile the cup was passed around. Such a ritual may have been insinuated by Luke (24,30); and the Eucharistic prayers given in the Didache

(9,1-10.5;14,1), in Justin (1,67) and in the Apostolic Tradition, indicate a similar form of prayer. Whether such a confraternity meal ever was considered as sacrificial is disputable. The comparison of the Last Supper to Jewish meals proposed by H. Lietzmann is skilfully rejected by J. Jeremias.[29] The closest parallel would perhaps be the meals of Qumran community. The members of the Qumran community blessed the bread and wine and distributed afterwards.[30]

According to Conzelmann,[31] although a certain Eucharistic meal existed, yet there is no evidence that it was the commemoration of Jesus. Conzelmann, however does not realize, as we have mentioned earlier, that the early Christians did not give evidence of having been a meal-community with long table talks in the very early stage. It is possible that the description of the Last Supper ceremony was inspired by the Passover, *Haburah, Zikkârôn* ceremonies. From this, however, it does not follow that the Last Supper was indeed essentially a Jewish passover, or any one of meal customs of the early decades of the first century. It was fundamentally a Christ event which pervaded and transformed the situation of the given time.

The question whether the Last Supper was a sacrifice, and what the very early understanding of it was, must be seen in the context of the sacrificial interpretation of Jesus' achievement. Since connected intimately with Jesus' death on the cross, its meaning cannot be separated from the historical understanding of the Jesus-event as sacrifice. In itself, the Last Supper cannot be considered as sacrifice. It is rather the beginning of the event which was accomplished on the Cross together with the resurrection which followed. This history of the Last Supper's interpretation as sacrifice leads to the question of the history of the sacrificial interpretation of Jesus' achievement in the life of the post-paschal community.

B. *THE PREHISTORY OF THE SACRIFICIAL INTERPRETATION OF JESUS' ACHIEVEMENT ITSELF*

As the result of our previous analysis of the theology of sacrifice in the different writings of the New Testament, we can say that the sacrificial interpretation of Jesus' achievement is rather a late development in the theology of the early Church. The Christ event was so unique that by itself it did not suggest any notion of sacrifice as it was known either in the Old Testament or in the pagan cultic religions. It was therefore an event which required both the application of a sacrificial terminology and at the same time a transformation of this terminology in its application. The sacrificial terminology resulted from the theological investigation of the relation between the will of God and the necessity of the death of the risen Christ. The sacrificial terminology seemed to answer the question why it was the will of the Father that the risen Christ had to suffer and die.

The early Synoptic pre-sacrificial theology was satisfied in saying that Christ had to die, because it was the will of the Father. Jesus was obedient to God even to his death, and God was pleased with the obedience of His Son. But when the further question was asked how God the Father could want the suffering and death of His Son, the sacrificial theology seemed to have the only satisfactory answer: God asked the death of His Son for the expiation of sin which offended Him and made Him angry and wrathful. This supposition is confirmed by the fact that the idea of sacrifice, remission of sin through expiation, and the notion of the anger of God appear together in the theology of Paul and of John as well. Paul seemingly was inspired by communities like those of Corinth, Ephesus and Colossae, centers of the Hellenic religious cults, and John and the author of the Letter to the Hebrews both belonging to priestly circles (cf e.g. 18.15), by familiarity with the sacrificial system of the Old Testament. The notion of sacrifice as meaningful answer for the question of why the Father willed the death of His Son evidently required a change or transformation in the notion of God as well. The Synoptic concept of pleasing God was to be if not replaced, certainly complemented by the concept of the wrathful God. Such a change might have been prompted by the frustration of the early Apostles in their apostolic work. The Good News of the resurrection and salvation was not accepted as promptly and universally as they expected. The notion of a revenging God was not only of great help in moving unbelievers to the acceptance of faith, but in explaining also the present sufferings and trials even to death which the faithful had to endure after having accepted the Good News of the risen Christ. The notion of sacrifice appeared to be helpful not only theologically but also pastorally in helping men to accept the will of God and at the same time in keeping them away from the Jewish or pagan sacrificial cults.

The foundation of the sacrificial interpretation was the absolute newness and incompatibility of Christ with the "old" time presented in the earliest stage of the Christian theology. This incompatibility meant also the exclusion of sin; however, it was much more universal and transcendental than sin. It did not mean only to forgive sins, but to bring new life and new happiness which transcends all the apparent values of the old time. The renewing power of the Christ event was understood so universally that no value, good or sinful, could escape its transforming force. The present was destined to pass completely, the early Christians thought, and the new future appeared as the only value which would last. Thus it seems that sacrifice in its embryonic form did not mean anything but the conviction and faith that the present visible world is relative, peremptory and the new and really valuable world is possible only by the virtue of God, whose way of life is to be accepted in faith and be preserved even at the risk of death. The Christ event, conceived in such a way was sacrifice, since it meant union with God. But unlike other religions, Christianity did not represent God as receiving man's gift under the symbol of ascending smoke. Rather, it is man who receives God, coming down to him in the form of a man. It was not a representative or vicarious sacrifice performed by the mediation of an animal, but directly by God who presented Himself in a self-revelatory event in order to be accepted by man in faith. In this sense not man to God but rather God can be said as sacrificing to man, i.e. uniting Himself to man. In other words it can be said that sacrifice was indeed nothing else but faith and obedience to the word of God.

If what we have said is true, it follows that the notion of the redemption in the Pauline interpretation of the Christ event was conditioned by the sacrificial interpretation rather than vice versa. The notion of sacrifice in Paul, understood as the reconciliation of God with men seems to be prior to the redemption. It is logical that once God is reconciled with man and accepts him, man becomes redeemed i.e. belonging to God, that is, a man *of* God. By considering the way of reconciliation as it was accomplished by God's only Son, Paul recognizes the great love of God for man, since He gave His Son for sinners. So it seems that the theological trend of Paul moves from justice to love (see Gal.Rom.Col.) as the meaning of Jesus' death. Jesus died according to the will of the Father because He wanted to reveal the gratuitousness of His love toward men.

Once sacrificial terms were applied to Christ and his work, it was not too difficult for Paul to extend such a terminology to the life of the faithful. It followed from his great theological principle sc. being in Christ. Once Jesus is seen as sacrifice (θυσία) it was at hand to extend the idea of sacrifice to the life of the faithful who were in Christ on account of their sharing of his life. Such an extension of the sacrificial terminology to the life of the faithful was not followed universally. The Johannine literature favors it less than the Pauline. A further extension of such a vocabulary to the breaking of bread took still more time (cf the end of the first century: Didache 14,1.2; Ignatius of Antioch Eph 5,2). Though the legitimacy of such an extension does not differ too much from the legitimacy of its application to the faithful, its usage depends on how closely the relation is seen to exist between Christ and the fact of breaking bread. Paul extended the sacrificial terminology to the faithful because of their union with Christ. Later he could recognize another very close relationship between the table and the cup of the Lord and the body and blood of Christ. He realized that any lack of distinction between the bread and cup of the Lord and any other bread and wine would be sin (cf 1 Cor 10,21-22;11,27-30), and as such cannot be expiated except by Jesus' death. Sin against the Lord's table cannot be forgiven except by Jesus' death. On the ground of such a relationship, neither sacrificial terminology nor effective remission of sin can be applied to the Eucharistic celebration independently of Jesus' death. But since bread and wine are so united with Jesus' body and blood, they are like words and symbolic expressions which can be applied to the symbolized reality as well as to the symbols. And this in a real sense, though it never happens independently of Jesus' death.

On the grounds of their relationship they can be interpreted in sacrificial terms, like Christ's achievement. The validity of the application of the sacrificial terms depends upon the understanding of the conjunction one makes between the related terms.[32] Thus the question of the real presence is connected with the validity of the application of sacrificial terms to the Eucharistic celebration.

There is a final question left. In addition to the early Church's interpretation of Jesus' achievement as sacrifice, is there any historical clue which would indicate that the historical Jesus too had some kind of awareness of giving his life for others and offering his life and death as sacrifice to God? The prehistory of the sacrificial interpretation of Jesus' work in the early Church leads to the question about the historical possibility of the historical Jesus' awareness and interpretation of his life and death as sacrifical.[33]

Notes

(1) For the suppositions of the undifferentiated pre-conceptual understanding which condition research in the idea of sacrifice in general as well as for the difference between the history of sacrifice and the theology of sacrifice with its threefold dimension see Horvath, T. "Prolegomenon to a theology of Sacrifice" in *Word and Spirit* Essays in Honor of David Michael Stanley, S.J. on his 60th Birthday, ed. by Plevnik, J., Toronto: Regis College Press, 1975, pp. 349-370.

(2) *From* (terminus a quo): the slavery of Satan (cf. expulsion of demons by Christ: Mk 3,22-30; Mt. 12,38; Lk 11,20, or by his disciples: Mk 3, 15;6,7;Lk 10,18), and that of sin (of remission of sins: Mk 1,27; Lk 1,77; Mk 2,1-22; Mt 9,1-8;Lk 5,14-26;7,48;24,47;Mt 16,19;18,19;cf Mk 14,22-25;Mt 26,26-28)

To (terminus ad quem): the presence of God (God the

Father, Son and the Holy Spirit is given: Mt 11,25-27; Lk 10,21-23; Mt. 26,26-28;Mk 14,22-25;Mt 28,20; Lk 11,13;22,19-20;Lk 12,21), peace (Mt 10.13;Lk 10,6) charity, (Mt 5,21-26.38-48),chastity (Mt 5,27-32), happiness and joy (beatitudes:Mt 5,1-12;Lk 6,20-23; wedding feast: Mt. 22,1-14;Lk 14,15-24;Mk 25,1-13; Mk 2,18-22; Mt 9,15; Lk 5,33-39;Lk 7,32-35;Mt 11,15-29;13,16; Lk 10, 24;10,20;Mt 25,34;Lk 22,30), and resurrection, eternal life (Mt 22,23-33;19,28-29;Mk 12,18-27; Lk 14,44;20,27-40)

Through the action of justification (Lk 18,13), regeneration (Mt 19,28) man is supposed to cooperate with God (cf Mk 4,20;Mt 25,1-13;24,42; Mk 13,37;Lk 12,40; Mt 25,1-13;24,42; Mk 13,37;Lk 12,40;Mt 25,31-46).

(3) *From* (terminus a quo): darkness (Col 1,13; 2 Cor 6,15), the power of Satan (Eph 4,26-27; 1 Tim 1,10;4,15; 2 Tim 2,26; 1 Cor 5,5), whose works are idolatry and sorcery (opposed to faith), concubinage, impurity, indecency, drunkenness and orgies (opposed to chastity), enmity, quarreling, anger, dissension, factions (opposed to charity and peace), envy, jealousy, selfishness (opposed to kindness and charity) (see Rom 1,24-32; 16,13-14; Gal 5,19-23): all these powers had been disarmed by Christ (Col 2,15;Rom 16,20; 2 Thess 2,8; Eph 6,12-16); and finally sin (as transgression: Rom 4,15;5,14;Gal 3,19; as delict: Rom 4,15; Gal 6,11; 2, Cor 5,19; as injustice: Rom 1,29; 1 Cor 13,6;2 Cor 12,13; as impiety: Rom 1,18; Tit 2,12; as iniquity: Rom 4,27; 2 Cor 6,14; Tit 2,14; and as power: Rom 5,12;6,6 with chapters 7-8) and Law (Rom 7,6 etc). The communion of light has nothing in common with this darkness (2 Cor 6,15).

To (terminus ad quem): a new relationship to the Father (God's belonging: 1 Cor 3,9; fellow citizen and member of the Father's household:Eph 2,13.19;1,5-9), to the Son (as Brother:Rom 8,29;Col 2,6-7; one with him in death:

Phil 3,10; one in resurrection:Eph 2,5;2,6;2 Tim 2,11; one in reigning in heaven: Eph 2,6;2 Tim 2,12; one in the same inheritance: Eph 3,6; Rom 8,17; one in promises: Eph 3,6; one in body:Eph 3,6) and finally to the Holy Spirit (Rom 5,5;1 Cor 12,7-8;2 Cor 1,22;7,5;Eph 1,17; 1 Thess 4,8; 2 Tim 1,7; man as His temple:Rom 8,9-11;8,17-39;1 Cor 3,16-17; 2 Cor 6, 16-17); new relationship also to the fellowmen (whom man has to love as God loves man: Eph 4, 32-5,1;Rom 13,8; and help: Rom 15,1;Eph 4,28) as well as to the whole comos (man has to bring it from the slavery of decay to the glory of sons of God:Rom 8,1-21); or in other words: peace (Rom 1, 7;15,13; Gal 5,2; Rom 14,17;15,23;16,20; 1 Cor 14,32;2 Cor 13,11:Eph 2,14;Phil 4,9;1 Thess 5,23;2 Thess 3,16) joy (Rom 14,17;15,13; 1 Thess 5,16;Phil 4,4), resurrection and eternal life (I Cor 15,1-28)

Through the action of rescuing and transferring (Col 1,14), of new creation (2 Cor 5,17;Gal 6,15), of regeneration (Tit 3,5), of resurrection (Eph 2,6;Col 3,1); of bringing to life again (2 Tim 2,11;Eph 2,5; Col 2,13), liberation (from old prisonment: Rom 7,6) of justification (1 Cor 6,11;Rom 3,20;Gal 3,11; Tit 3,5-7), of sanctification (Rom 6,19; 1 Cor 1,30;6,11;1 Thess 4,3-7;5,23;1 Tim 2,15;4,5), of reconciliation (Rom 5,10-11;2 Cor 5,18-20)

(4) *From* (terminus a quo): sin (Jn 1,29;20,13;1 Jun 1,9;2, 12;3,5;4,10), death, hatred, lies, murder (Jn 8,44-45), the works of Satan (1 Jn 3,8)

To (terminus ad quem): communion with God (1 Jn 1,3), the Father (Jn 14,23), the Son (Jn 3,16;6,27.32-33) and the Holy Spirit (1 Jn 3,24;4,13;Jn 14,16) and being one with God as the Father and Son are one (Jn 15,5;6, 57;14,20;17,22;1 Jn 2,24-25; cf Jn 15,1) and with the fellowmen (1 Jn 1,3) giving life for them (1 Jn 3,16-17); also peace (Jn 16,33;20,21), plenitude (Jn 1,15), joy (Jn 15,11;16,22;17,13), resurrection for eternal life (Jn 6,

40.50.54;8,51;3,16;6,27.40.51.54.58;10,28;11,25-26) being begotten by God and having His seed within (1 Jn 3,9) *Through* the action of regeneration (Jn 1,13;3,3;1 Jn 3,1-10;5,1.18), of liberation (by making man free: Jn 8, 32.36), of passing out of death into life (1 Jn 3,14), of purification (1 Jn 1,7-9), ablution (Jn 1,29;1 Jn 3,5) expiation (1 Jn 2,2;4,10) and cancelling of sin (Jn 20, 13;1 Jn 1,9;2,12).

The author of the Epistle of Barnabas describes Jesus' work as leading his people out of the old world into a "new promised land of milk and honey" - 6,11-19;Funk, F.X., *Patres Apostolici,* I. Tübingen, Libraria H. Laupp, 1901, pp.54.56.

(5) αἷμα (means of salvation): Mt 26,28; Mk 12,24; Lk 22,20; Jn 6,53; 6,54.55.56;Acts 20,28; Rom 3,25;5,9; I Cor 10,16;1 Cor 11,25.27; Eph 1, 7;2,13; Col 1,20; Heb 9, 12.14.25.57; 1 Pet 1,2.19; 1 Jn 1,7;5,6; Rev 1,5;5,9;7,14;12,11; 19,13.

ἀμνός (slaughtered without opening his mouth) Jn 1,29.36; Acts 8,32

ἀμνός (Paschal Lamb) 1 Pet 1,19; the idea without the term: Jn 19,36

ἀρνίον (Paschal Lamb) Rev 5,6;13,8

θυσία Eph 5,2;Heb 7,27;9,23;9,26;10,12

θύω 1 Cor 5,7

θυσιαστήριον Heb 13,10

ἱλασμὸς Rom 3,25;Heb 2,17;1 Jn 2,2;4,2

Πάσχα 1 Cor 5,7

προσφορά Eph 5,2;Heb 10,10.14

προσφέρω Heb 5,7;7,27;9,14.25.26.28;10,12

(6) ἄζυμος 1 Cor 5,7

αἷμα (cause of defeating Babylon)Rev 17,6;18,24 (with 19,2;6)

ἀρνίον Jn 21,15

93

θυσία   Rom 12,1;Phil 2,17;4,18; Heb 13,15.16;1 Pet 2,5

σπένδωμαι   Phil 2,17;2 Tim 4,6

(7) αἷμα   (cup) Mt 26,27-28;Mk14,23-24;Lk22,20;1 Cor 10,16;11,25.26.27.28;(drink)Jn6,53.54.55.56; 1 Cor 11,25.26.27.28

ἀρνίον   (supper of the Lamb) Rev 19,9

τράπεζα, 1 Cor 10,21 (cf Heb 9,2)

(8) There is some probability that the Jewish Akedah (the binding of Isaac: akedat Yishak) served as model for Paul to understand how God could allow the suffering of His Son. Rom 8,32 is a reminiscent of Gen 22. In Rom 5,8-9 Paul uses the *a fortiori* form of argument; cf. Nils, A. Dahl, "The Atonement, An Adequate Reward for the Akedah? (Rom 8,32)" in: Ellis, E.E., Wilcox, Ed. *Neotestamentica et Semitica*, Studies in Honour of Matthew Black. Edinburgh: T.T. Clark, 1969, pp.15-29.

(9) Cf Sabourin, A., *La Rédemption Sacrificielle*, Montreal: Desclée, 1961, pp 183ff.

(10) Such an interpretation solves the problems concerning the variant reading (the Church of God or the Church of Christ) and concerning the grammatical understanding of τοῦ ἰδίου. It takes the more usual reading (the Church of God) and refers to Jesus' blood as God's own on account of the relation existing between God and His most own Son. Moreover it makes unnecessary the unlikely usage of the *"communicatio idomatum"* among the two divine persons by calling the blood of Jesus, blood of the Father.

(11) It seems that 1 Cor 11,25-26 by stressing the idea of inseparability accentuates the idea of real presence more than the concept of the sacrifice inasmuch as this latter would mean only some sort of giving up oneself for someone (cf "given for many" in the Synoptics)

94

(12) Admitting this idea of sacrifice the question whether the historical Jesus could have interpreted his life achievement as sacrifice can be answered by the historian positively. Evidently a historian can never know for sure what a man like Jesus who did write nothing about himself had thought of himself 2,000 years ago. Nevertheless he can establish some conditions necessarily connected with data properly documented. That Jesus visiting the temple or celebrating Paschal meal did think of himself as symbolized by the sacrificial victims is psychologically possible but extremely difficult if not impossible to demonstrate historically. Supposing the dogmatic tradition of the Church concerning the special knowledge and beatific vision which Jesus as God-man had, one would admit that he did see himself as victim for the remission of sins. To admit, however, this as a necessary condition of his historical situation is a completely different matter.

Omitting here the details, let us suppose with R. Bultmann that Historical Jesus proclaimed the Kingdom of God at hand ("The Primitive Christian Kerygma and the Historical Jesus" in: Braatan C.E. and Harrisville, R.A. ed. *The Historical Jesus and the Kerygmatic Christ,* New York: Abingdon,1964, p.23). Once proclaiming this Jesus had to be aware of the consequences i.e. of being harassed and of being put in the power of his adversaries. The fact of proclaiming the Kingdom of God is at hand implies an awareness of being dedicated to do the will of God at any price. This dedication to do the will of the Father is reflected in Jesus' uncompromised character which bothered somewhat the early Church. In fulfilling the will of the Father, Jesus could recognize that the new being incompatible with the old will demand the destruction of the old. The subsequent interpretation of the purpose of his life could detect both the placation of angry "affectus" of God and the expiation of sin, the "effectus" of wrath of God (see Footnote 17) as implied in Jesus' dedication to do the will of the Father.

(13) The New Testament sacrifice is essentially oriented not so much to perfect the cosmical world, but man in his internal "ethical" life. In this sense it is much more consistent with the Old Testament theology (fundamentally original) than the Old Testament sacrifices (borrowed from neighbouring people). New Testament horizon of understanding for sacrifice is not the past (like cycle-repetition of past events in many Non-biblical religions) and not even the future to come (cf. Old Testament messianism) but the present in which the future proleptically is already active by liberating the present from the past. Or in other words the sacrifice of the New Testament is demanded by the inevitability of the resurrection. It is a progressive attitude which includes a radical dissatisfaction with the present world and a conviction that the new risen life is more valuable than the surrounding present. The New Testament sacrifice has a proper pattern which is the man's realization in the light of the new world of the resurrection, necessarily transcending the actual one and which in the light of the same resurrection appears as relative and peremptory.

(14) Marxsen, W., *The Lord's Supper as Christological Problem,* tr. by L. Nieting, Philadelphia: Fortress, 1970.

(15) Marxsen, W., *op. cit.,* pp. 21-22.

(16) The Last Supper can be seen as a "declaratory formula" by which Jesus, like the priests of Old Testament sacrifices, declares what kind of sacrifice is the one which is going to be offered; cf Ringgren, H., *Sacrifice in the Bible,*

London, Lutterworth, 1962 p. 28; cf Rad, G. von, *Old Testament Theology*, New York: Harper, 1962, I, pp. 246-247; 261-262.

(17) Many New Testament scholars are puzzled by seeing the reappearance of the wrath of God in Pauline writings. In order to remove from the Pauline theology the rather anthropomorphic notion of an angry God, they propose the distinction between wrath of God as personal "affectus" of God and wrath of God as impersonal "effectus" (see D.E.H. Whitely, *The Theology of St. Paul*, Philadelphia: Fortress Press, 1966, p. 61-72). The term, they claim, is to show not how God feels, but rather how His power acted in ordering history. Now whereas such an interpretation can remove from Pauline theology an anthropomorphic notion of God, it will not necessarily remove an anthropomorphic theologizing process. It must be admitted that both the notion of the "wrath of God" and that of sacrificial expiatory interpretation appear jointly in the post-Synoptical writings of the New Testament. This incidence should not be dismissed without consideration. It would be uncritical to suppose that the set "wrath-expiation" is purely accidental. The two terms, especially in the writing of St. Paul have a theological function. This remains true even if the effective sense of the "wrath of God" is exclusive for Paul. The fact that Paul did talk about the mercy of God as well as the anger of God supports the view that unlike the Synoptics, Paul tried to explain Christ event not only in a personal and ethical but in sacrificial sense as well.

Moved from the same concern as the so called effectist school, C.H. Dodd *(The Epistle of Paul to the Romans, 1932, 12th edition. 1949, London: Hodder and Stoughton, pp, 54-57)* and S. Lyonnet *(De Peccato et Redemptione* II, Rome: Pontificio Instituto Biblico, 1960, pp. 97-117) explained the word ἱλαστής in twofold sense: to placate a man or God and to expiate sin. As expiation it would mean not so much placating an angry God, but annulling guilt. Such an interpretation is legitimate but fails to explain why had been the notion of ὀργὴ τοῦ Θεοῦ and the cultic sacrificial interpretation Christ event introduced together in the post-Synoptic writings of the New Testament. To reduce the wrath of God as an "effectus of God" as love (see Whiteley, *op.cit.* p.72) speculatively it is very sound, but exigetically too simple. More particularly if one considers that outside the Book of Revelation Paul is the only one who applies θυμός to God (Rom 2,8) a term which he applies to human passion (e.g. 2 Cor 12,20; Gal 5,20; Eph 4,31; Col,3,8)

(18) Instead of reviewing the ongoing discussion in Redaction Criticism we point out those data and contexts which challenge many assumptions and which are to be taken into consideration in future research.

(19) 4 Macc, 18,4; cf Bruce, F.F., *The New Testament Development of Old Testament Themes,* Grand Rapids: W.E. Eerdmans, 1968, pp 99.

(20) *Isra* and *idma* in Aramean or *basar* and *dan* in Hebrew. The Synoptics use σῶμα whereas John σάρξ cf Jn 6,51-56, since for him σῶμα means rather corps, dead body: cf 19,31.38.40; 20,12.

(21) Dupont, J., "Ceci est mon Corps, Ceci est mon Sang," in: *NouvRevTheol* 80 (1958) 1023-1041.

(22) Such an interpretation is supported by a Palestinian antecedent. According to Targum Neofiti Codex found in Vatican Library by A. Diez Macho in 1956, bread is referring not to an object but to a person. It is said, that he (Moses) is the bread given by the Lord to eat (see Vermes, G., "He is the Bread, Targum Neofiti Exodus

16,15," in: Ellis, E.Z., Wilcox, M. (ed.) *Neotestamentica et Semitica*, Edinburgh: T.Clark, 1969, 254-263).

(23) *Ant. Jud.* 2,14, par. 3

(24) Boismard, M.E., "Christ the Lamb, Redeemer of Man," in: Sheets, J. E. (ed.) *The Theology of the Atonement*, New Jersey: Prentice-Hall, 1967, p. 160; translation of the article in: *Lumière et Vie* 7 (1958) 91-104.

(25) Lyonnet, S., "The Pauline Conception of Redemption," in: Sheets J.E. (ed.) *op. cit.* p. 179; *Lumière et Vie* 7 (1958) 35-66.

(26) Jaubert, A., *The Date of the Last Supper*, trans. by I. Rafferty, Staten Island: Alba House, 1956 (French ed. 1957).

(27) Jeremias, J., *Eucharistic Words of Jesus*, trans. by N. Perrin, London: SCM, 1966. p. 24-26; see also Benoit, P., *Exégèse et théologie*, Paris: Cerf, 1960, pp. 255-264; Lohse, E., *Die Geschichte des Leidens und Sterbens Jesu Christi*, 1964, Gütersloh, pp. 48ff. Eng. tr. *History of the Suffering and Death of Jesus Christ*, Philadelphia: Fortress, 1967.

(28) Leenhardt, F.J., *Le sacrement de la sainte cène*, Paris: Delachaux et Niestlé, 1948; Thurian, M., *The Eucharistic Memorial; I The Old Testament, II The New Testament*, tr. by J. G. Davies, London: Lutterworth, 3rd ed. 1966; Lietzmann, H., *Mass and Lord's Supper. A Study in the History of the Liturgy*, tr. by D.H.G. Reeve, Leiden: Brill, 1953-69; Marxsen, W. *op. cit.*

(29) Jeremias, J., *Eucharistic Words . . .* pp. 29-31.

(30) Kuhn, K.G., "Über den ursprünglichen Sinn des Abendmahls und sein Verhältnis zu den Gemeinschaftsmahlen der Sektenschrift," in: *EvTheol* 10 (1950-51) pp. 508-527.

(31) Conzelmann, H., *An Outline of the Theology of the New Testament*, tr. by J. Bowden, London: SCM, 1969, pp. 53-54.

(32) This is what the Council of Trent intended to do by calling the Eucharistic celebration a real sacrifice. It forgives sins not as bread and wine but as being separate from any other bread and wine and related to the body and blood of Christ who died as sacrifice for the remission of sins. Since there is real remission of sins in the Mass, the Mass is a sacrifice. The definition of sacrifice was seen by the Fathers of the Council of Trent as something forgiving sins and the Mass did this though not by itself but by its relation to the sacrifice at the Cross.

(33) See footnote 12. The question of historical possibility of the historical Jesus' awareness and interpretation of his life and death as sacrifice is connected with the question of the historical possibility of his awareness of his faith-raising power in himself. See Horvath, T., *Faith Under Scrutiny,* Notre Dame: Fides, 1975, pp. 125.132-133,142ff.